TAMING
THE
BIG BAD
WOLVES

Also by Joy Wilt

TAMING THE BIG BAD WOLVES

How to Take the Huff and Puff Out of Twelve Parenting Problems

JOY WILT

WORD BOOKS

PUBLISHER
WACO, TEXAS

ISBN 0–8499–0063–8
Library of Congress catalog card number: 78–65801
Printed in the United States of America

*I would like to dedicate this book to
Marilyn Patterson (my sister and friend).*

*(Without Marilyn, a few of the Big Bad
Wolves would have gobbled me up long ago!)*

Acknowledgments

I would like to thank the following people for making the Big Bad Wolves in my life a whole lot easier to take!

Thanks to Bruce (my husband), Christopher (my son) and Lisa (my daughter), whose encounters with the Big Bad Wolves are recounted in the pages of this book.

Thanks to:
    Ron Berry (my brother and business manager)
    Sally Cummins (my friend, personal manager and business associate)
    Ted Cummins (my friend and business associate)

Thanks to my editors:
    Janet Gray
    Pat Wienandt

Thanks to the following resource people:
    Dan and Carol Barker
    Phyllis Hart

Joyce Heatherly
Ernie and Faith Hergenroeder
Rennie Mau
Connie McCleary
Rita-Lou Reid
Betty Takeuchi
Joe Venema
Bill and Terre Watson

And last but not least . . . thanks to the publishing team at Word Books. Without them, you would have to cope with the Big Bad Wolves minus the help of this book!

Contents

Foreword

WHO'S AFRAID OF THE BIG BAD WOLVES? All of us are—and that's as it should be!

Throughout life there are problems that each of us inevitably must face. These problems have dangerous potential to influence us negatively—to "eat us up." I call them "big bad wolves," and taming them is a process that needs to be learned early in life.

How does one escape the negative influence of the big bad wolves? Not by running—they will catch us every time! Not by seeking shelter in so-called "safe" places—big bad wolves have been known to blow down houses made of straw and sticks. Even brick houses aren't completely safe, because sometime or another, we'll have to come out.

The way to handle a big bad wolf is to change the nature of the beast so that his influence is positive rather than negative.

Big bad wolves are notorious for eating up little children. They come knocking on the door, disguised in a variety of ways and calling, "Little child, little child, let me come in!"

Some parents teach their children to shout back at the wolf, "Not by the hair of my chinny chin chin!" But parents who understand the nature and the potential of big bad wolves take a firm hold of their child's hand, open the door and greet the wolf with, "Why, Mr. Wolf, please come in—we've been expecting you! We've got a lot to talk about!"

Teaching children how to cope with the Big Bad Wolves— that's what this book is all about.

Introductory Remarks

Many parents are skeptical of "parenting books." Very often the people who write these books are out of touch with children and with reality. I feel that this is not the case with me.

I have worked with children (birth through twelve years of age) from all races, religions and socio-economic backgrounds for the last fifteen years. As a result, I am quite aware of the fact that there are no perfect parents and there is no perfect approach to parenting.

If this book is not to present a formula for perfect parenting, then what does it do?

My objective in this book is to offer guidelines and suggestions that will help parents become facilitators. I firmly believe that *it is not the job of a parent to control his child's life. Instead, a wise parent helps his child get in control of his own life. This is done by manipulating the environment instead of the child.*

Barking out orders or issuing edicts doesn't work. Neither

does it work to let a child do whatever he wants, whenever and wherever he wants. Both ends of the parenting spectrum are dangerous. I know, because I've been there! Somewhere in between complete authoritarianism and total permissiveness lies the key to successful parenting. There is room for all kinds of parents and all kinds of parenting philosophies in the "middle of the road."

One last word before you begin: For those who are offended because the English language uses the generic *man* when it means person, let me say that because I am not aware of any acceptable alternative, I consistently use the words *he, him,* and *his* throughout this book to indicate either or both genders. This is done in accordance with our present language structure and is in no way to be construed as representing a belief that men are superior to women.

MONEY

1. Money—The Root of All . . . !

Only three more shopping days until Christmas and, according to past experience, there were only three more days until my checking account would go into overdraft. Nonetheless, in the true "spend, spend, spend spirit of Christmas," my daughter Lisa and I were out doing some last-minute shopping.

We had gotten caught in a traffic jam caused by the holiday rush, and because there was only one hour left before the stores would close for the day, everyone was uptight. Christmas carols were resounding over the car radio and Lisa was joining in, at the top of her lungs, a little off-key and several beats behind. " 'Tis the season to be jolly," she sang, while I tried hard to squelch the urge to scream "Humbug!" Other fellow "traffic jam participants" were not as concerned as I was about preserving the holiday spirit, and they began honking their horns and screaming obscenities out the windows of their cars. Amid the many sounds of Christmas, Lisa stopped singing (thank goodness!) and spoke up.

"I'd like to have a new jacket, a fuzzy one like Leah's!" she stated.

"What's the matter with the one you've got on?!" I snapped.
Lisa pouted: "It's not fuzzy!"

With the sound of a cash register ringing in my imagination, I shouted, "Well, fuzzy or not, it's in good shape, it fits and it keeps you warm."

"But it's not fuzzy!" Lisa insisted.

By this time the traffic had begun to move, and although our car was slowly going forward, I was standing firm. "Sorry, Lisa, I'm not getting you a new jacket!"

"But why?" she sobbed.

"Because," I answered, "I'm fresh out of money!"

There was a long pause and then Lisa spoke up. "But Mom, you don't need any money to buy me a jacket. Just write the store one of those notes or show them one of your cards, and they'll give you the jacket for free!"

It took me awhile to realize exactly what Lisa was referring to, but I finally figured it out. Lisa was talking about my checks and credit cards. It had never dawned on her that the checks I wrote and credit cards I used represented money. She didn't realize that the bills I sweated over at the end of every month related to the "notes I was writing and the cards I was showing."

That did it! If Lisa was ever to know and understand that it took money to buy things, I was going to have to teach her; and so among my many New Year's resolutions I included a commitment to lead both of my kids into an understanding of money.

Getting Children Interested in Money

It took us a little while, but before long Bruce and I formulated our strategy. We finally concluded, after much discussion, that if Chris and Lisa were to understand and value money they needed to have their own. So we decided to give each of them a weekly allowance. Because we didn't want them to think that "money grew on trees" we felt that it was best to keep their allowances modest.

I got my first clue that our little project was going to be a long haul when Chris refused the first installment by saying, "No, thanks, I don't need it." Lisa added to my anxieties when she looked at the money we gave her and asked, "What's this for?"

It was back to the drawing board for Bruce and me. Our project had just begun and already we had encountered our first valuable lesson about kids and money. *A child must want or need money before he will be motivated to understand it.*

Up to this point we had spoiled our children rotten. Not wanting to deprive them, we had overindulged them with everything their little hearts desired. They did not need or even want anything . . . including money.

Well, needless to say, the entire Wilt household was in for a drastic change—one that would be tough on the adults as well as the kids. The kids liked getting but probably not half as much as we liked giving. In a sense, Bruce and I had gotten caught up in the whole "our-kids-are-going-to-have-every-thing-we-never-had" syndrome, and the losers, believe it or not, were the kids.

Our first step was to curb our own spending. No more letting the kids slip things into the shopping cart at the super-market. No more doling out money for the show every time they had an invitation to go. No more buying "little things" just because a friend had one or because it was advertised on TV as something no kid could live without.

We replaced our overindulgence with, "If you want it, you'll have to buy it yourself." You can imagine how that went over!

Tantrums and other forms of pouting began to prevail. In the weeks that followed, we heard it all: "But so-and-so has one. Why can't I have one?" "You're the meanest mom I know!" "You're selfish!" "How come you can buy anything you want and I can't buy anything at all?" "Gee whiz, it doesn't cost very much!" "Cheapskate!" And so on, and so forth.

There were times when Bruce and I seriously questioned

whether or not we'd make it through the pass—but heroically, we hung on.

It took a while, but after what seemed like a forever, Chris and Lisa began to catch on. I got my first clue that they both were coming around when they began counting their money periodically to make sure that it was all there.

The Need and Desire for Money

So far, I've told you how I got into the whole money issue with my own kids. All of my efforts up to this point in my personal story were directed toward getting my children interested in money. For me this was quite an accomplishment. I've heard of children who were born with a natural inclination toward using money, but I've yet to meet one. Most of the kids I know have had to come through the process Chris and Lisa came through before they were motivated to learn about money. It seems to me that a need or a desire for money usually precedes the desire to know about money.

This is why I begin my "Every Kid's Guide to Making and Spending Money" classes with a discussion of "Why do people need money?" I've been involved in a lot of these discussions and, generally speaking, the children I've worked with give answers like these:

1. Money makes it possible for people to buy some of the things they need and want.
2. Money can help people do the things they want to do.
3. Money can help make people's dreams come true.
4. Money can help a person express his love and appreciation for another person.
5. Money can make it possible for a person to help other people.
6. Money can help a person get in control of his life (or, as one student put it, "Money can help you be your own boss").

One of the first things a child will ask when he becomes

aware of what money can do for him is, "How can I get some?" We discuss that question in our classes too and are pretty well agreed on several ways a child can get money.

Finding Money

In every money management class there's at least one child who has a phenomenal story to tell about the time he found some money. It's always fascinating to watch the child who is telling the story, but it's even more fascinating to watch the children who are listening. "Now, that's my style!" a listener exclaimed at the end of one such story. Everyone in the class giggled and applauded. Many children fantasize about finding a fortune in the gutter—but it's to be hoped that they don't count on it. Sooner or later they've got to come to grips with the fact that getting money usually requires hard work.

Incidentally, before we move on to the second way children can get money, let me say that whenever I hear of a child finding money (or anything else, for that matter) I encourage the child to try to find the owner before deciding to keep it. If a child has diligently tried, without success, to find the owner, he will feel much better about keeping the money than if he had assumed the old "finders keepers, losers weepers" attitude right off the bat.

Monetary Gifts

A second way children can get money is to receive it from someone as a gift. Again, this is nice, but I tell kids, "Don't depend on gifts to keep you adequately supplied with money."

A lot of adults feel funny about giving children money instead of games, equipment, toys or clothing, but if a child enjoys using money, nothing could be greater. Money, when given to a child who appreciates and knows how to handle it, makes a marvelous gift.

Sal, one of my students, put it this way. "Whenever people ask me what I want for my birthday or for Christmas, I tell them money, because I know that when I get it I'll be able to say, 'Just what I always wanted!' " Sandra, another student, said, "I ask for money because I know I'll not have to take it back to the store to exchange it."

Allowances

A third way children can get money is through an allowance. I define an allowance as being a child's share or portion of the family income. Generally speaking, parents do not tell their children that they will have to forego meals or sleep outside if they fail to do certain chores. In most families it is automatically assumed that every family member is entitled to a certain amount of space and a certain portion of the family's possessions. This is where the allowance fits in. An allowance is not something that a child earns. It is something that he receives because he is a member of the family.

Cheers and applause usually resound whenever I tell this to the children in my money management classes. But alas, the accolades fade away when I go on to explain that:

"Sharing with the family" means sharing the family's responsibilities as well as its possessions. A family, like any other group, can give to its members only as it receives something in return.

Thus, children who receive from the family must put something back into it.

How do I as a parent decide what my child's share of the family possessions should be? This is the first question most parents ask when they are trying to decide on an amount for their child's allowance.

To decide how much money you are going to pay your child, decide how much money you have and give him an appropriate share. Some parents have found that giving their child a percentage of their net income works out very well.

The advantage of sharing with children on a percentage basis is that whenever money is available the children get some. Whenever money is not available, the children (like the parents) have to do without.

"Our children receive a percentage of our income for their allowance," a parent once told me, "and it works out very well. You see," she continued, "my husband is a salesman and the kids automatically know that when daddy's check is big, their allowance is big. Conversely, when daddy's check is small, their allowance is small. This whole system really paid off when my husband was out of work for six months. The kids never asked for their allowance because they knew that a percentage of nothing was nothing."

In regard to how much of a percentage you should give your child, I've known some parents to give their children as much as 10 percent of the family's net income. However, a greater number of families have settled on 1 percent.

Obviously, the exact percentage must be left up to each individual family.

Before you make your final decision about your child's allowance, I strongly recommend that you consider the following:

1. Your child's maturity and his ability to handle money. You may have noticed that I did not say "your child's age." This is because I feel that ability and maturity do not always coincide with a child's age. I've known some very young children who were extremely adept at handling money. Conversely, I've known some adolescents who were inept money-managers. This is not to say that good money-management skills cannot be learned. Indeed, if you are hesitant about giving your child money because of his maturity or money-management abilities, you may want to consider helping your child acquire an understanding of money rather than waiting for him to understand it on his own.

2. Your child's needs.

3. Your child's desires.

4. How much money your child's peers have. The child who is the "spoiled kid on the block with money to burn" has just as many problems as the "poor kid on the block who never has any money." Both situations lead to social encounters that involve feelings of jealousy, rejection, rivalry, and more. This is tough—especially for children who have not yet learned how to cope with these kinds of feelings. Thus, it is important to try, as much as possible, to avoid making your child the one in his group who is the "odd ball." Find out how much money your child's friends receive and take this into consideration when you are deciding how much your child should have.

5. What your child will be responsible for buying. Obviously, the child who is responsible for buying all of his clothes, school supplies, lunches, etc., should receive more money than the child who only has to buy supplementing snacks and supplies. Some parents find it easier on everyone involved when their children are responsible for "everything." Other parents do not agree. Whichever approach you feel comfortable with, *before* any money is dispersed, be sure to spell out exactly who is responsible for buying what. Also, you may want to post in a conspicuous place a list which spells all of this out. This precaution can ward off many arguments regarding money.

As you consider each of these things, remember that it is extremely counterproductive to underpay children. If a child does not receive enough money in one way or another to support the things he needs or wants, he may become discouraged and give up, or, worse still, he may resort to unethical ways of obtaining money. Either way, everyone loses.

This is not to say that parents are responsible for providing their child with an allowance that covers their child's every want or need. No way! Children must depend on themselves as well as their parents for the money they need or want. This is why we encourage children to supplement their allowance and the money they receive as gifts with "extra earnings." The next chapter will deal with the subject of extra earnings.

SUMMARY

A. A child must need or want money before he will be motivated to understand it.

B. Children need to understand money if they are to respect and value it.

C. Children recognize several reasons why a person may need or want money:
   1. Money makes it possible for people to buy some of the things they need and want.
   2. Money can help people do the things they want to do.
   3. Money can help people's dreams come true.
   4. Money can help a person express his love and appreciation for another person.
   5. Money can make it possible for a person to help other people.
   6. Money can help a person get in control of his life.

D. Children can get money by:
   1. Finding money. This does not happen very often, but when a child finds money he should be encouraged to try to find its owner before deciding to keep it.
   2. Receiving monetary gifts. Money, when given to a child who appreciates and knows how to handle it, makes a marvelous gift.
   3. Receiving an allowance. An allowance is the child's share or portion of the family income, not something a child necessarily earns. In deciding exactly how much allowance a child should receive, parents should consider:
      a. How much income the family receives.
      b. The child's maturity and his ability to handle money.
      c. The child's needs.
      d. The child's desires.
      e. How much money the child's peers have.
      f. What the child will be responsible for buying.

2. Making It

"Under no circumstances will I allow my son to work! He's entirely too young," a father once told me. "When I was a kid," he continued, "I had to work. I missed out on a lot—my whole childhood, to be exact—and I'm not going to let the same thing happen to my son."

I could understand why this father was so adamant about his son not working. To him work was drudgery and the perfect childhood was one in which there was little or no responsibility. Unfortunately, many people share this man's misconceptions. I call them misconceptions because the children I've worked with through the years have proven that work can be a joy and responsibility can enhance a child's life.

A good example of what I'm talking about is the motto that my first money management class came up with:

> We'll pretend it's play
> But we'll work all day
> to get the dough we need
> to buy our toys and feed.

The same group decided upon the following group pledge:

Whatever we do,
We've got to like doing it, and
It's got to make money.

Not all of my money management classes developed mottos
and group pledges, but all of them were extremely resourceful. It is from these groups that I gathered the following list
of suggested money-making projects for children. Each suggestion has been tested and proven to be successful.

If you have a child who needs or desires more money than
gifts or his allowance provide, you may want to share the
following ideas with him.

There are two basic ways a child can earn money:

1. He can sell something to someone else.
2. He can do something for someone else and be paid for
   his services.

Earning Money by Selling Things

If a child wishes to earn money by selling something, he
could sell:

Something he owns
Something he has collected
Something he has made
Something on consignment.

A child who decides to sell something he already owns may
consider selling:

His old toys, games, and equipment
Clothes he has outgrown
Old Hallowe'en costumes
His old records and tapes
His old magazines, books, and comic books
Pets (old ones or babies produced by the old ones)

A child who decides to sell something he has collected may consider selling:

> Old newspapers (sell them to a recycler)
> Seashells and starfish
> Rocks and minerals
> Bark and decorative tree twigs and branches
> Seeds, pods, pine cones, dry weeds, and flowers
> Mistletoe
> Bottles (some can be returned to the store for a refund, others can be sold)
> Coupons (from newspapers, magazines, cereal boxes, mailers)
> Fresh flowers
> "Good" junk (reusable discards)
> Fresh fruit and vegetables (these can be grown or picked —with permission)
> Old clothes (to use for Hallowe'en costumes or dress-up)

A child who decides to sell something he has may consider making and selling:

> Fruit juice (lemonade, orange juice, grape juice or punch)
> Beanbags
> Homemade cakes, cookies, and candies
> Sundaes, sodas, popsicles, and other sweet treats
> Macramé pieces
> Potholders
> Aprons
> Boxes
> Drawstring bags
> Green plants (start them from cuttings or seeds, then sell them after they have grown)
> Handmade stationery and cards
> Candles
> Tie-dye T-shirts, scarves, etc.
> Puppets

Bird feeders
Sandwiches
Terrariums
Pottery
Pressed dry flowers
Leathercraft
Patchwork
Toys

A child who decides to sell something on consignment may follow this basic procedure:

Find someone who wants to sell something he owns.

Find someone else to buy the object.

If the child sells the object, he gets to keep some of the profit. (The exact amount should be agreed upon ahead of time.)

If he doesn't sell the object, he should return it to the owner at no expense to the child.

A yard or garage sale is a very good way to sell things on consignment.

Earning Money by Providing Services

A child who likes to do things indoors can:

Inquire at a local store if someone is needed to do some straightening or cleaning up.

Take care of someone's indoor pets and plants while he is away on vacation. Someone may also be needed to turn lights on at night and collect newspapers and mail.

Water and care for his parents' house plants.

Pack the family's lunches.

Do mending and sew buttons onto garments that need them.

Polish someone's silver or brass.

Clean and polish shoes.

Clean and wax furniture.

Prepare a simple meal for the family and clean up afterwards.

Help clean up during and after parties.

Help someone do "spring housecleaning."

A child who likes doing things outdoors can:

Ask at a local store if he can have a job running errands and/or making deliveries.

Clean and vacuum the inside of cars.

Wash the outside of cars.

Paint someone's outdoor furniture.

Offer his parents an "on-call" errand service, running errands whenever needed.

Sweep the pavement of his street and ask for a small donation from each house.

After heavy snows, shovel paths and driveways.

Paint people's house numbers on the curb in front of their houses.

Mow lawns.

Rake leaves.

Weed flower beds.

Walk other people's dogs.

Clean animal pens and horse stables.

Harvest fruits and vegetables.

A child who likes working with people younger than himself can: (Please note: **The child should get permission from his parent and the younger child's parent before he does any of these things.**)

Take a baby for a ride in his stroller or baby carriage.

Watch toddlers while they play in the sprinkler.

Take a child to the park to play.

Take a child to the library, helping him choose books and following up to make sure that the books are returned to the library on time.

Escort a young child to and from school.

Keep a child occupied and entertained while his mother does other things in or around the house.

Help a mother plan and put on a birthday party for her
child.

Keep a child occupied and entertained while his mother
rests.

A child who likes working with older people can:

Read newspapers, magazines, books, or letters to them.

Write letters for them.

Do their marketing.

Run errands and make deliveries for them (for example,
take their mail to the post office).

Help them prepare meals and clean up afterwards.

Escort them on walks.

Help them with their housecleaning.

Help them keep up their lawns, gardens, and the outside
of their house.

A child who likes to perform or entertain people can do one
of the following, inviting his family, relatives, friends, and
neighbors to these events and charging admission:

Put on a magic show with homemade magic tricks.

Put on a story hour for younger children.

Put on a "dress-up" fashion show.

Develop a professional clown or monster costume and
make appearances at birthday parties and other special
events.

Put on a variety show.

Put on a play or a puppet show.

A child who likes doing things that are somewhat out of the
ordinary can:

Start a rental service, renting his toys, games, and equipment to anyone he knows will take good care of them.

Repair broken toys and then sell or rent them.

Produce a neighborhood newspaper and sell it to people
in the neighborhood (include neighborhood news,
riddles and jokes, announcements, want ads, etc.).

Write, and possibly illustrate, a book. Include interesting
things about people in his family, neighborhood, or

school. Make copies of the book; then sell it. People
who are mentioned in the book will be his best market.

Take pictures at home, church, school—anywhere—and
sell prints to the people he's photographed. (Parents
are especially interested in pictures of their children.)

Bathe someone's dog.

Repair bikes.

Open a gift-wrapping service (especially profitable during the Christmas holidays.

Decide what subject he excels in and tutor kids who are
having trouble with that subject in school.

Umpire or referee at neighborhood games.

Put on a pet show, a hobby show, or an art show, giving
awards (certificates or ribbons) to the participants
and charging admission to the show.

Make a spook house and charge admission to it.

Basic Steps to Earning Money

Whatever your child decides to do, his efforts are more
likely to succeed if he follows the eight basic steps which I tell
the children in my money management classes:

Step One: Decide what you would like to do.

As you make this decision, consider these three things:

1. What do you enjoy doing?
2. What can you do well?
3. What do people who will be paying you (your family, relatives, friends and the people in your community)
   want or need?

You can determine what people want or need by doing one
or all of the following:

1. Look around and see if you can discover things that
   need to be done.
2. Talk to people, in person or by telephone.
3. Distribute a questionnaire (a sheet of paper with questions on it), in person or by mail. Here is a sample questionnaire:

If the following goods and services were available inexpensively in your neighborhood, how often would you purchase them? Put 1 for once or more a week; 2 for once or twice a month; 3 for once every two or three months; and 4 for less often than that.

___Yard care—weeding, mowing, watering

___Toy and play equipment rental and repair

___Custom-made macramé pot hangers

___Window washing

What other goods or services would you like to see available in your neighborhood?

Step Two: Do research. Find out.
1. How to do what you would like to do.
2. How much your project will cost.
3. How much time your project will take.

You can do your research at the library or you can get information and advice from other people.

Step Three: Get permission from your family to do what you want to do. Make sure that what you want to do will not impose on your parents or other family members.

Step Four: Learn how to do what you have decided to do.
1. If you are going to make something and sell it, learn how to make a good enough product for people to buy.
2. If you are going to do something for someone and charge for your services, learn how to perform your duty well.

You can learn a skill by doing research at the library or you can have someone teach you the skill.

Step Five: Decide on a fair price for your product or service. As you make this decision, consider these three things:
1. How much money will the project cost?
2. How much time will the project take?
3. What will people be willing to pay?

You should not overcharge (charge too much) because you will not be able to sell your product or service. You should not undercharge (charge too little) because you will lose the time and money you have put into the project. You may want to ask an adult to help you determine prices.

Step Six: Advertise (let people know about) your product or service. Try any or all of the following:

1. Put an ad in the local newspaper.
2. Put ads on bulletin boards in local stores, community centers, laundromats, etc.
3. Post a sign in front of your house or in other appropriate places.
4. Have a flier printed up (a sheet of paper which has all of the necessary information on it) and then distribute it in person or by mail.

Step Seven: Sell your product or service. Talk to people in person or on the telephone; or, if you have enough money, you can pay someone else to help sell your product or service.

Step Eight: Deliver your product or service.

1. Make sure that you deliver on time.
2. Make sure that you deliver everything you promised to deliver.
3. Make sure that everything you sell is in good condition.
4. Make sure that everything you do is your best effort.

SUMMARY

A. Work can be a joy, and responsibility can enhance a child's life.
B. There are two basic ways a child can earn money.
   1. He can sell something to someone else.
   2. He can do something for someone else and be paid for his services.
C. If a child wishes to earn money by selling something, he could:

 1. Sell something he owns.
 2. Sell something he has collected.
 3. Sell something he has made.
 4. Sell something on consignment.
D. If a child wishes to earn money by providing services and getting paid for them, he can:
 1. Work indoors.
 2. Work outdoors.
 3. Work with people younger than himself.
 4. Work with older people.
 5. Perform for or entertain people.
 6. Be creative and do something out of the ordinary.
E. Whether a child sells something or offers a service, there are eight things he should do to make sure that his efforts make money.
 1. Decide what he would like to do.
 2. Do research (find out what he would like to do, how much the project will cost, and how long it will take).
 3. Get permission from his family to do what he wants to do.
 4. Learn how to do what he has decided to do.
 5. Decide on a fair price for his product or service.
 6. Advertise (let people know about his product or service).
 7. Sell the product or service.
 8. Deliver the product or service.

3. Spending It

It was early Saturday morning. I had gone to the church where I worked to do some last-minute preparations for Sunday. I hadn't been in my office for more than fifteen minutes when my door flew open, and there in the doorway stood John. "I blew it!" he announced angrily. "I blew every cent of it!" I knew immediately what John was talking about. He had worked all summer long and had earned over $400. Some he had spent on camp, some he had spent on school supplies— but what about the rest? "I went to Arrowhead with my Aunt Laura and Uncle Bill and my two cousins," he told me. "We spent a lot of time at the penny arcade, and—" Mid-sentence, John paused. There was a long silence, and then he concluded: "It's gone! Every cent of it!"

John had encountered a harsh reality of life: the improper management of one's money can cause a lot of grief. The old "easy come, easy go" adage is little comfort to a child who has worked and saved for a long time only to end up with a few short memories.

This is why I feel that equipping a child with money-making skills is only half the battle. Money-management skills are equally important.

Teaching children money-management skills begins with an explanation of exactly what can be done with money. I tell my students that there are three things that they can do with money. They can:

1. Save it.
2. Give it away.
3. Spend it.

Managing money wisely usually involves all three of these things.

Saving Money

Remember Bank Day at school? Maybe you're not old enough to have experienced it, but when I was a kid, every Wednesday was Bank Day. On Tuesday each child was given a 3" × 5" manila envelope with his very own savings account book in it. The next day he brought the envelope back to school with the savings account book and some money (usually a quarter) enclosed. The bank would pick up the envelopes, deposit the money, and record the deposit in the savings account book. It was a clever idea, but for some reason (probably the fact that many quarters never made it to school) the program was dropped.

Anyway, this was my first exposure to saving money, and I distinctly remember how I responded to the whole thing.

Collecting the "numbers" (the record of deposits) in your bank book was a big deal. It was a prestigious thing to have a book that was filled with numbers. I remember that. But I also remember that even though it was fun to compare bank books, I always wished I had kept all the quarters I had "given" to the bank. To me, at that time, putting the quarters in savings was like giving them away, and a bank book filled with numbers was little consolation for never having any spending money. The man in the corner market who had the neatest assortment of penny candy in town was totally unimpressed with the fact that my bank book had more numbers in it than anyone else's at school!

Thus a savings account for children who do not understand it, or for children who do not have very much money, is sometimes counterproductive. A good old-fashioned "piggy bank" is my recommendation for a $10 to $20 savings plan. There are several good things about saving money this way.

To begin with, the child who drops money into a piggy bank experiences first hand what saving money is all about. He can see what happens when money is added to an account and left there.

Another good thing about this method of saving money is the feeling of pride, accomplishment, and ownership that the child experiences when he possesses his own money.

Money saved in a piggy bank is easily gotten to when it is needed—unless, of course, the bank is a tricky one that can't be gotten into. I don't recommend banks of this kind because they're frustrating. In addition, they don't require the self-discipline that needs to be developed if a child is ever to save money on a larger scale.

And then there's the pleasure a child derives from counting his own money. For some reason, counting real money seems to be more exciting for children than looking at the balance in a savings account book.

All in all, the piggy bank is a handy thing.

But what about children who have more than $20 to save? This is where the bank comes in. It's too risky to keep more than $20 lying around the house. I've heard a lot of strange and sad stories about piggy banks that have been lost or stolen and, unfortunately, in most cases, the loss represented the sum total of the child's savings.

So if your child decides, either on his own or because of adult encouragement, to begin a savings account, help him in any way you can. I say, "help him," but try not to do it for him. The more a child does to begin and maintain his own savings account the better off he'll be. Many of the children I've worked with have even gone so far as to provide their own transportation (via bikes and skateboards) to and from the bank.

Before I leave the subject of saving money, I want to answer an important question: "How much money should a child save?" Again, this depends upon each individual child, how much money he has, and whether or not he's saving money for a specific project. The children I've worked with seem to feel comfortable with saving 10 percent of their total income.

But however much your child decides to save, I recommend that he save neither too little nor too much of his total income. Too much money into savings leaves too little for spending. Too little into savings doesn't add up fast enough to motivate the child to continue saving. Either way, the child experiences a great deal of frustration and usually ends up thinking that saving money is a crummy idea.

"I'm saving up for college," a little girl told me in the bank one day. It was Friday evening and the bank was jammed with people. I was standing in back of the little girl who had spoken to me. "Oh," I responded, "that's nice! Where do you think you'll go to college?"

The little girl looked puzzled and then said hesitantly, "I'm not sure exactly what college is!" I was taken aback for a moment and then, without thinking, I asked, "Then why are you saving your money to go to college?" Quickly she answered, "My mom and dad make me. They say I'll thank them for it some day." There was a pause in the conversation and then the girl spoke again. "I may thank them some day, but I don't thank them now—I'd rather keep my money and use it for something I want."

With college tuition as high as it is today, I sincerely question whether or not a child could ever save enough money to make a dent in what is needed. In my opinion, parents who cannot afford to foot the bill for college are better off equipping their children with the skills they need to work themselves through college. Forced savings for something the child does not understand or want often has a negative effect.

Like the trick piggy bank, a forced savings plan does not require the self-discipline that needs to be developed if a child is to save money on his own for the rest of his life.

Saving money should be voluntary. A good way to encourage a child to save money is to suggest that he save for something specific. At first, I feel he should avoid saving for "big things," because, if what he's saving for costs a great deal of money in proportion to his total earnings, he may become discouraged and give up. This is especially true if the thing he is working for is so far out of reach that he never attains it.

Saving money becomes a rewarding thing only when children can, in some concrete and tangible way, see the fruits of their frugality and patience.

Giving Money Away

"Can a child be taught to give something away?" a young mother once asked me.

"I believe that a child can be taught the motions of giving something away," I answered, "but the 'spirit of giving' has to come from within."

The classic example of this was a young boy I knew who was forced to give some of his candy to another boy. "I'll give Carl some of my candy," he said, "but I'll wish that I wouldn't have done it!"

It is true that this boy went through the motions of giving, but the giving spirit was obviously missing.

How does this relate to children giving money either to individuals or to organizations? Giving at its best happens when the person who is giving is motivated to do so. Feelings such as love, responsibility, respect, appreciation, and gratitude will quite naturally motivate a child to give. But, generally speaking, these feelings exist only in the context of a relationship. Thus, if the giving spirit is to abound, a positive relationship must exist between the giver and the receiver. Giving in any other context is often superficial and meaningless.

This is why I feel that it is counterproductive to force a child to give something to someone or something else. If he is not naturally motivated to give, he may give with resentment and hostility, and this is good for neither the giver nor the receiver.

"The Lord loveth a cheerful giver—but He'll take it any way He can get it!" a minister once joked from the pulpit. His statement may have been clever and funny, but I questioned its validity. I've come in contact with people who gave money to the church out of a sense of guilt or because they honestly believed that God would somehow increase their income if they gave. All too often these feelings of guilt and/or anticipation of increased income are transferred to the children in the church and they function accordingly. Quite often these same children become disillusioned when they overcome their guilt or discover that tithing does not necessarily double their monetary income. When this happens, their giving stops. This is a tragedy for both the child and the church.

Children who are allowed to develop an understanding of the church and a relationship with it before they tithe are more likely to give their money in the right spirit. Granted, this takes time. Meanwhile, I explain tithing to children by telling them:

The money you give to an organization that helps other people is called a "donation." In order for an organization to receive donations, it must be one that does not make money—a non-profit organization. The Red Cross, the Community Chest, Goodwill Industries, and the Salvation Army are just a few of the non-profit organizations that receive donations and use the money to help other people.

A church is a non-profit organization that helps other people. If the donation you give to your church is 10 percent or more of the money you earn, it is called a tithe. Giving a tithe to your church is a good thing for you to do.

Your tithe will be used to keep your church going so that it can inspire, educate, and help the people who attend it. Your tithe may also be used to help people who do not attend your church.

Giving money away either to individuals or to organizations is a good thing to do, but only when the money is given with a positive spirit and attitude that comes from within.

In keeping with this attitude I feel it is somewhat counter-productive to give children money to put in the offering plate on Sunday morning. This activity often becomes meaningless to both parents and children because the gift does not truly come from the child.

Spending Money

"Spending money is the funnest part of having it," a boy once told me. Very few people would disagree. Spending money is fun—especially when you know how to do it right.

This is precisely why so much time in my money management classes is spent on budgeting. I always begin this segment of the course by asking the class what the word *budget* means. I get all kinds of interesting answers. Here are just a few.

"A budget is a small piece of fudge candy."

"That's what you do when you need to move something. You budge it."

"A budget is numbers and writing on lined paper."

"My mom buys our food and clothes with her budget instead of money."

"It's the list Dad makes of all the bills he gets in the mail."

It is true that I've received some pretty clever and creative responses to my question, but very few children have been able to come up with an accurate definition of the word *budget*.

The definition I offer to children is that "a budget is a plan for spending money." I elaborate this concept by telling the children that:

A budget lists a person's
    Income (how much money he has), and
    Expenses (what he plans to use his money for).
His expenses should include:
    Savings (how much money he plans to save)
    Donations (how much money he plans to give away, including his tithe)
    Needs (what he needs to buy)
    Wants (what he wants to buy)

Here is a sample of the budget sheet I encourage my students to use:

Budget for the week of _____

Income

Allowance	_____
Extra earnings	_____
Other	_____
Total income	=========

Expenses

Savings	_____
Donations	_____
Needs	_____
Wants	_____
Total expenses	=========

After the word *budget* is defined and explained, I go on to tell the children:

Regarding expenses and income: If your expenses add up to more than your income, you're in trouble. You should not spend more money than you have. When your expenses are more than your income, you can do one of two things: You can either make more money to add to your income, or you can give up some of the things you want to buy.

Regarding needs and wants: Think about what you need and want; then buy the most important things first. This is called "prioritizing."

To prioritize the things you are going to buy, make a list of everything you need. Next, rearrange the list, putting the most important things at the top of the list and the least important things at the bottom. Then buy things in the order in which they appear on the list.

Regarding buying things: Think about what you are buying before you buy it. Buy things that do what they are supposed to do. Make sure that they really work. Buy things that are not already damaged or broken. Make sure that the things you buy are well made and sturdy enough to resist being damaged or broken. Buy things that are safe. Do not buy things that could hurt you or someone else.

Make sure you pay a fair price for the things you buy. This may mean that you have to look in several stores before you buy what you want.

Buy things from a store that has a good reputation—one that will assume responsibility for the things they sell you.

If you have any doubts or questions about something you are going to buy, talk to your parents before you buy the item.

Generally speaking, a great deal of satisfaction can be derived from managing money wisely, for it is true that money, just like so many other things in life, when gotten fairly and used properly, can be a wonderful thing.

SUMMARY

A. There are three basic things that can be done with money, and managing money wisely usually involves all three. A person can:

1. Save it.
2. Give it away.
3. Spend it.

In regard to saving money:
A. There are two basic ways for a child to save money.
   1. The "piggy bank" (for $10 to $20 accounts)
   2. A bank savings account (for $20-and-up accounts)
B. Forced savings are counterproductive as they do not require the self-discipline that needs to be developed if a child is to save money on his own for the rest of his life.
C. Saving money becomes rewarding when children can see in some concrete, tangible way the fruits of their frugality and labor.

In regard to giving money away:
A. Children can be taught the motions of giving something away, but the "spirit of giving" has to come from within.
B. Giving at its best happens when the person who is giving is motivated to do so.
C. Children who are forced to give either to individuals or organizations often do so with resentment and hostility. This is good for neither the giver nor the receiver.

In regard to spending money:
A. A budget is a plan for spending money. It usually lists a person's
   1. Income (how much money he has), and
   2. Expenses (what he plans to do with his money).
B. Children should
   1. Budget their money and avoid spending more money than they make.
   2. Prioritize the things they are going to buy.
   3. Consider carefully what they are going to buy before they buy it.

BOOKS FOR CHAPTERS ONE, TWO, AND THREE

If your child begins to show some interest in money, you may want to refer him to one or all of the following books:

Dozens of Ways to Make Money, Yvonne Michie Horn.

Good Cents: Every Kid's Guide to Making Money.

How to Turn Lemons into Money, A Child's Guide to Economics, Louise Armstrong. New York: Harcourt Brace Jovanovich, 1976.

A Kid's Guide to Managing Money, Joy Wilt. Waco, Tex.: Educational Products Division, Word, Inc., 1979.

The Kids' Money-Making Book, Jim and Jean Young.

Money and Kids, Mary Price Lee.

My Allowance and How I Use It, Jon M. Taylor. Berkeley, Cal.: The Ideal System Co., 1972.

My Bank Book, Learning about Money and How to Use It, Gail Mahan Peterson. Kansas City, Mo.: Hallmark.

4. Pitching In and Sharing the Load

Company was coming, and they were due to arrive any minute. Frantically, I was rushing around the house taking care of last-minute details. I went to put something in the trash bag under the kitchen sink only to discover that it was full and overflowing. "This will never do!" I thought to myself, so in desperation I called out, "Will someone please empty the trash bag under the sink?"

It didn't take long to get my first response. "It's Lisa's turn to do it!" Chris yelled.

"No, it isn't!" Lisa retorted. "I emptied it the last time!" By this time both kids were nose to nose in the hall.

"But I emptied it two times before that!" Christopher insisted. With that Lisa blurted out some offensive remark and Chris responded with a jab to her left arm.

The doorbell rang just as I arrived at ringside to break up the fight. There was no time for a lecture on the importance of brothers and sisters getting along. "Go to your rooms and cool off," I demanded. Whining and pouting, the children dragged themselves into their rooms. Bruce went to the door to greet the guests and I rushed back to the kitchen to empty the trash. "It's just not fair!" I moaned to myself as I made my way to the trash can. "How come I always end up having to do everything myself?"

The answer to my question was simple. I did everything myself because I didn't make my children assume the responsibility that was theirs as members of our family. Do you know why? Simple. I would rather have done things myself than hassle with my kids. This is because I could do a job in half the time it took me to get my kids to do it. And by doing the job myself I saved wear and tear on my nerves—or so I thought.

But what about my self-concept and my whole sense of justice? Was doing everything myself good for me? Was it good for my children? Was it good for our relationship? Of course not! This fact led me to reevaluate what was happening around our house. Bruce and I were doing everything, and the kids were getting off scot free! It was time for a family meeting!

One evening we all sat down together and talked about family responsibility. "You never do anything around here!" I complained. Chris jumped to his feet and Lisa leaned forward in her chair. "What do you mean!?" Chris shouted. "Yeah!" Lisa added, "what do you mean? I've been dressing myself every morning and even combing my hair!" "And I've been cleaning my own room!" Chris said.

The children were right. They had been assuming more and more responsibility in regard to themselves and their personal belongings. But what about doing things to contribute to the general welfare of the family? That's what *I* was talking about.

Family Responsibilities and Jobs

Whenever two or more people live together, it is important that everyone contribute something to the group if it is to survive and grow. In chapter 2, I talked about children taking from the family. I advocated that children are entitled to receive a portion of the family's possessions. Now I want to expose the other side of the coin—the "giving" side.

If children are to receive from the family, which they automatically do by eating, sleeping, and living with the family, they should be expected to give something to it.

To decide exactly what each member of the family should give and when he should give it, I recommend the following:

1. Gather the entire family together.
2. Make a list of every responsibility and job that needs to be done in and around the house. (You may want to check your family's list with the following list to make sure that you have included everything. Also refer to the lists in chapter 2 of this book.)

Indoor chores:

Straighten "community areas" (areas shared by the entire family).

Sweep, vacuum, mop, wax floors.

Dust, polish furniture.

Empty trash cans.

Wash, fold, iron, put away clothes.

Scrub sinks, toilets, tubs, basins.

Prepare meals.

Set the table, clear the table.

Wash, dry, put away dishes (or load and unload the dishwasher).

Wash walls and woodwork.

Outdoor chores:

Weed, mow, trim yard.

Wash windows.

Wash outside of house.

Sweep walks.

Vacuum, wash, wax car.

Rake leaves.

Straighten and sweep the garage.

Straighten and sweep the patio or porch.

Put full trash cans out, bring empty trash cans back.

Shovel snow from walks.

Miscellaneous chores:

Gather the mail and the newspaper.

Run errands.

Baby-sit.

3. Carefully go over the list and decide which jobs should be "paying jobs" and which jobs should be "non-paying jobs."

4. Begin two charts, like the ones shown below. Entitle the first chart "Family Responsibilities," and in the column marked "Responsibility," list all of the "non-paying" jobs.

FAMILY RESPONSIBILITIES

Responsibility	Person responsible	When the responsibility is to be done

Entitle the second chart "Jobs that Pay Money." List all of the paying jobs in the column marked "Jobs."

JOBS THAT PAY MONEY

Job	Amount of money to be paid for job

5. Finish the "Family Responsibility" chart by deciding:
   a. Who will be responsible for what responsibility.
   b. When the responsibility is to be done.
   c. What consequences a family member will have to suffer if he does not complete his responsibility (you may or may not wish to include this on the Family Responsibility Chart—it's up to you and your family).

When completing the Family Responsibility Chart, you'll need to take into consideration the age, ability, and preferences of each family member. You will also need to consider how much available time each person has to give to the family.

Make sure that you do not "overload" any one family member, especially young children. Start out slowly with a young child. Give him a few simple responsibilities; then add to his load as he proves that he can handle the jobs he has been assigned.

6. Finish the "Jobs That Pay Money" chart by deciding how much money will be paid for each job. Take into consideration how much money is available, how much effort the job requires, and how often the job will need

to be done. Refer to chapter 2 for more information on this subject.

7. Post both charts in a conspicuous place (the refriger-ator door is my family's favorite spot).

8. Evaluate both charts as often as necessary. Add new responsibilities and jobs as the family approves them and drop obsolete ones.

Incidentally, "trading" jobs and responsibilities is a fair thing to do as long as both of the people involved in the trade are satisfied with the outcome.

Also, paying another family member to perform your job or assume your responsibility is fair. If a child has enough financial resources and initiative to pull this off, I say, "More power to him!"

This system really works—and it works well if parents are consistent and children are encouraged to "follow through."

Training Children How to Do Chores

"What's the matter with the way I did it?" Lisa demanded, whenever I remade her bed. In the beginning, Lisa loved doing chores herself, but this didn't last long! This was not because of Lisa; it was because of me. It was I who couldn't stand the lumps and wrinkles left in her bed whenever she made it!

This proved to be detrimental. I got my first clue that some-thing was wrong when, one morning, out of sheer desperation, I asked Lisa to make her bed. Guests were knocking on the door and there was no time to be picky. "Why should I make my bed?" Lisa asked sarcastically. "You'll just do it over again!"

And so I learned my first valuable lesson regarding children and chores: do not expect perfection from children.

With this in mind, let's start from the beginning. To teach your child how to do a specific chore, try following this simple procedure. I call it the "Show Me How, Then Let Me Do It" method.

1. Demonstrate how the task should be done by doing it yourself while your child watches.
2. Do the task together or encourage your child to do the task while you watch him. (Avoid criticizing his efforts and praise anything he does correctly while you are watching.)
3. Let him do the task alone.
4. Praise his work and express appreciation for what he has done.

Your child's bedroom is a good place to start using this method.

Teaching Children How to Straighten and Clean Their Room

As indicated in the preceding paragraph, it is useless to *tell* your child to clean up his room if you haven't taken the time to show him how.

Organization is a skill that needs to be learned. It is not something that a child automatically knows.

If you are going to show a child how to straighten and clean his room, you may want to use the following guidelines.

1. Make the bed.
2. Pick up anything that is out of place and put it on the bed. To do this, start from a specific corner of the room and work out from that point.
3. After the furniture and floors have been cleared, pick up each item on the bed one at a time and put it in its proper place.
4. Dust the furniture (start from one corner of the room and work out from that point).
5. Vacuum or sweep the floor (again, start from one corner in the room and work out from that point).

And now for the "Show Me How, Then Let Me Do It" method:

Let your child watch you clean his room one time. The next

time, do the job together. After this, your child should be able to clean his room on his own. The first few times he cleans his room on his own you may need to give him some verbal assistance, but you shouldn't give him much more. If you do, he'll keep trying to get you "actively involved" every time he cleans his room.

Incidentally, if you want your child to maintain his room, you need to help him organize it so that *everything has a place*. Don't encourage your child to "stuff" things. This means don't let him be content with "getting things out of sight." Things that are not in their proper place can cause a lot of frustration and anxiety. Admittedly, I have a fetish about everything being in its proper place, but this is only because I value them. Things that are misplaced take *time* to relocate. In addition, misplaced things do not get used as much as they should. This can be a waste. So if you want to do everyone a favor, try to get organized and encourage your child to do the same.

Using the "Show Me How, Then Let Me Do It" method, you can teach your child how to do almost anything!

"When can I start?" one enthusiastic parent asked me. "Is my four-year-old old enough?" "He certainly is!" I answered. Of course, every child is different, but most children are ready to start assuming responsibility when they are around two years of age. A child this old will not completely "earn his keep," but he can begin to "share the load." By doing small jobs and by assuming more and more responsibility for himself and his possessions, he can be a real help. If you're a young mother who has been feeding, dressing, and picking up after a child for two years, you know what I mean.

In any case, don't wait too long to get your child involved. If you don't want to be left holding the bag (trash bag, that is), make sure that every member in your family is doing his part to "tote that barge and move that bale!"

SUMMARY

A. Whenever two or more people live together, it is important that everyone contribute something to the group if it is to survive and grow.

B. If children are to receive something from the family, they should be expected to give something to it.

C. To decide exactly what each member of the family should do and when he should do it.

   1. Gather the entire family together.

   2. Make a list of every responsibility and job that needs to be done in and around the house.

   3. Go over the list and decide which jobs should be "paying jobs" and which ones should be "non-paying jobs."

   4. Begin two charts:

      a. Entitle the first chart "Family Responsibilities."

      b. Entitle the second chart "Jobs That Pay Money."

   5. Complete the "Family Responsibilities" chart by deciding

      a. Who will be responsible for what responsibilities.

      b. When the responsibility is to be done.

      c. What are the consequences of unfulfilled responsibilities.

   6. Complete the "Jobs That Pay Money" chart by deciding how much money will be paid for each job.

   7. Post both charts in a conspicuous place.

   8. Reevaluate both charts whenever necessary.

D. In regard to children and chores: Do not expect perfection from children.

E. The "Show Me How, Then Let Me Do It" method can be used to teach children how to do chores.

   1. Demonstrate how the task should be done by doing it yourself while your child watches.

   2. Do the task together or encourage your child to do the task while you watch him.

    3. Let him do the task alone.

    4. Praise his work and express appreciation for what he has done.

F. If you want your child to maintain his room, you need to help him organize it so that everything has a place.

G. Most children are ready to start assuming responsibility when they are about two years old.

BOOKS FOR CHAPTER FOUR

In regard to family responsibilities, the best book I can refer your child at this point to one of my series of *Ready-Set-Grow* Books: *The Nitty Gritty of Family Life* (Waco, Tex.: Educational Products Division, Word, Inc. 1978).

5. "Not Until Your Homework Is Done!"

"No playing outside and no watching TV until your homework is done!"

Sound familiar?

If you have a child in school, chances are you've said this more than once, and chances are you've experienced all the hassles associated with homework.

Homework . . . a necessary evil? I know plenty of kids who'd agree with the "evil" part of this statement, but what about the "necessary" part?

Personally, I am not sure that homework is a necessary part of a child's education. That is why I advocate doing away with it. I will deal with my reasons for feeling this way in the second part of this chapter. As for now, what if your child is part of a system that insists on loading children up with homework? What should you do?

How to Handle Homework

I recommend that you arrange a conference that involves you, your child and his teacher. Make it clear during the conference that you will not be responsible for your child's homework. Let *both your child and his teacher* know that completing homework assignments is your child's responsibility and collecting them is his teacher's responsibility. Indicate that you will be willing to help your child if and when he asks you to, *but* make it clear that you will not check up on him or force him to do his homework.

This will place the responsibility where it needs to be placed, and it will keep a lot of unwarranted pressure out of the relationship between you and your child.

Then when your child shouts, "Mom,"—or "Dad," whichever the case may be—"I'm home!" avoid asking him about his homework and issuing a bunch of threats. Greet him with a hug instead!

"Just what do you have against homework?" a parent asked me. "Plenty!" I answered. From the very beginning of my years as a teacher, I resisted sending work home with children, but school policy and parental pressure won out and I joined the ranks of the so-called "good teachers who care enough to give homework."

Then one day one of my third-grade students approached me: "Parents get to leave their work at the office, but children have to bring their work home. How come?" Unable to come up with a decent answer, I decided right then and there that homework wasn't fair.

In an attempt to correct the situation, I announced that homework assignments would be given to only those students who were unable to complete their work during the school day. Naturally, my students were thrilled, but their parents seemed ready to tar and feather me.

It was obvious that a parent-teacher meeting was in order. So I sent notes home with my students inviting their parents to the school. They lost no time responding, angrily demanding that I explain exactly what I had against homework.

Luckily, I was prepared. This is what I told them.

The Disadvantages of Homework

Day after day, children drag their tired bodies home from school, only to be greeted at the door, not with love but with negatives—no playing and no TV until homework is finished. Look at it from a child's point of view. After spending almost six hours behind a desk, is it any wonder that he balks at returning to one for one or two more hours? "Enough is enough!" he screams, and can we really blame him?

In my opinion, six to eight hours a day, five days a week is enough time for any child to be in school. Thus, my number one complaint against homework is that it unnecessarily extends a child's school day. This problem often leads to others.

Something inside every child tells him that he needs to play—and whatever that something is, it is right! Everyone needs to play if he is to survive and grow. Play is essential to life! When a child is doing homework, he is *not* playing. And so we come to my second complaint. Homework often interferes with the play, rest, and relaxation that children desperately need in order to live healthy, normal lives.

"But couldn't you give our kids homework that is fun to do?" one parent asked.

"Let's talk about that!" I said. "Homework of any kind is a structured activity. Of course a certain amount of structure is good, but engaging a child in structured activities on a continual basis can be extremely counterproductive. Unstructured play and socializing enhance a child's creativity. In addition, they contribute to a child's mental, emotional and social growth." Homework that replaces unstructured activities stands the chance of inhibiting a child's growth and development. Herein lies my third complaint.

My fourth complaint involves a child's responsibility to his family. All too often I've had parents brag to me, "My child's education is so important I do his chores so that he can do his homework!" What a rip-off! This is not fair to the child and it is not fair to his family. As members of a family, children need to assume responsibility (see chapter 4). Of course, there will be times when a legitimate excuse prevents a child from doing a particular chore or responsibility, but this shouldn't happen on a regular basis. Nothing, including homework, should completely replace a child's responsibility to his family.

Then there's the frustration children experience when they have two adults teaching them the same concept. "But that's not the way my teacher explained it," children complain after their well-meaning parents explain how to do a math problem. It can get pretty confusing to a child to have a "new math" problem explained in "old math" terms.

Thus, school work done at home often complicates and even inhibits the educational process. This is my fifth complaint.

Complaint number six is: Homework often becomes a major source of conflict between parents and children—as though children and parents didn't have enough problems to solve!

"Is it worth it?" I asked the parents at the meeting that night. It was quiet for what seemed like a forever, and then one of the fathers spoke up. "You know," he said, "I'm glad you have decided to do what you are going to do. I'm sick of fighting with John over his homework!" A second father agreed. "Now maybe all of us can get some rest and relaxation!" There were some smiles and even a few chuckles. Several parents enthusiastically shook my hand on the way out the door. I had won more than a battle; I had won the war, and from that day on, as far as my classes were concerned, school work was confined to school.

SUMMARY

A. In situations where homework is an inevitability, parents need to make it clear to their child and his teacher that:
  1. Completing homework is the child's responsibility.
  2. Collecting homework is the teacher's responsibility.
  3. The parent will be available upon request to help the child, but will not check up on the child or force him to do his homework.
B. There are several reasons children should not be given homework.
  1. Homework unnecessarily extends a child's school day.
  2. Homework often interferes with the play, rest and relaxation that children desperately need in order to live healthy, normal lives.
  3. Too often homework replaces the unstructured play and socializing that are vital to a child's mental, emotional and social growth.
  4. Homework often prevents a child from fulfilling his responsibilities to his family.
  5. School work done at home can complicate and even inhibit the educational process because children often receive different explanations from parents and teachers.
  6. Homework often becomes a major source of conflict between parents and children.

6. Dynamite Duds

It was four days before Lisa's third Easter. Proud of myself that I had finished my shopping several days early, I hung her Easter dress along with its accessories on the outside of the closet door. Smugly, I sat on the edge of the bed and admired my selections. Everything right down to the hair barrettes matched perfectly. In addition, the coordinating shoes, purse, hat, and gloves were the cutest I had ever seen! Lisa was sure to be the darling of the parade on Easter Sunday morning!

"Isn't it simply gorgeous!" I said enthusiastically to Lisa as she entered the room. She glanced at the outfit, took a moment to examine the hair barrettes and then announced, "It just isn't me!" With that she snipped her nose up and headed toward the door.

"Hold it!" I screamed. "Exactly *what* do you mean it isn't you?"

"Mamma," she said solemnly, "you never buy things with curls and I look so good in curls!"

"Curls!" I thought to myself. "Since when did they start making dresses with curls?"

I flashed on the several "seldom worn" outfits that hung in Lisa's closet. I had successfully forced her to wear them on a few occasions, but the knock-down-drag-out fights it took to get her to cooperate were hardly worth it.

The only thing I could think of was the money that would be wasted if Lisa decided that this new outfit didn't suit her fancy.

Angrily, I yanked the dress off of the hanger and stuffed it into a shopping bag. "Well, then," I yelled at Lisa, "it's obvious that my choice in clothes isn't good enough for you! So let's see how well you can do on your own!"

I dragged Lisa along with the dress back to the department store where I got it.

"We need to exchange this dress," I told the sales clerk.

"Oh?" she questioned, as she scrutinized the merchandise I was returning. "And what shall I say is the reason for the return?"

"My *daughter* doesn't like it!" I answered. Undaunted by my negative attitude and the clerk's hesitation to make the exchange, Lisa left my side and began wandering up and down the aisles, looking at each dress on every rack.

"Shall we help your daughter select a new dress?" the clerk asked.

"Not on your life!" I retorted. "This is one selection Lisa is going to make on her own!"

"Perhaps we should help her with the size?" the clerk persisted.

"No, thank you!" I responded, and with arms folded, I stood impatiently tapping my foot on the floor.

It wasn't long before Lisa surfaced from the racks with a dress draped over her arms. "This is it, Mamma!" she exuded. "I found my Easter dress!" I grabbed the dress out of her arms and checked the size. Surprisingly enough, it was the right one. Pointing her to the dressing room, I said coldly, "If you're big enough to pick out your own clothes, you're big enough to get your own self dressed."

Unfazed, Lisa made her way to the dressing room. Soon

she appeared, dressed in the garment she had chosen. It was long and had a full, flouncy skirt. She spun around. "Oh, Mamma," Lisa squealed with delight, "it goes out so far!" Then looking in the mirror, she pointed at the ruffles that lined the bottom of the dress. "And look, Mamma, it has curls!"

The dress Lisa had chosen was nothing that I would have selected; I am much more into tailored styles. But after watching Lisa prance around the store for a few minutes, I realized that her selection was really right for her. In fact, I finally broke down and admitted that she had made a marvelous choice.

Needless to say, we bought the dress and took it home. This time it was Lisa who insisted on displaying it on the closet door.

When Easter day finally rolled around, Lisa was up at the crack of dawn getting dressed. At 9:30 she waltzed into her Sunday School class. "Oh, Lisa," her teacher gushed, "you look absolutely beautiful. I just love your dress!"

"Thank you!" Lisa said proudly. "I picked it out myself!"

This was not the only compliment Lisa received that day, or other days. There were many more, every time she wore her Easter dress (which was quite often).

I always wondered whether it was the dress that drew the compliments or the way Lisa looked in the dress that made people respond so positively. Whichever it was, the whole ordeal had taught me a valuable lesson. *More important than how a child looks in an outfit is how he feels in it.*

Parents can make a value judgment about the way a child *looks* in an outfit, but only the child himself can say how he *feels* in it.

This is why I think it is imperative to let children help select their own clothes.

Preparing to Shop for Clothes

But parents shouldn't pull back completely. Children need to have a framework in which to function if they are to make wise choices regarding their wardrobes. To help a child choose his clothes wisely, I suggest that you consider doing the following:

Before you take your child shopping:
1. Check with your child's school to see if it has any dress codes or regulations. If it doesn't, ask for suggestions or recommendations regarding the way your child should dress. It may be a good idea to take your child along with you when you gather this information. Then he will get it "straight from the horse's mouth" and you will not be blamed for decisions made by the school.
2. Check out the stores in your area. Make a note of the ones that sell clothes in a price range compatible with your budget.
3. Let your child know at least one day in advance that you will be going shopping. Prepare him for the fact that it may take one whole day to complete his wardrobe.
4. Make a list of everything your child will need to get in order to complete his wardrobe. Include shoes, socks, underwear, etc.
5. Let your child know approximately how much money you will be spending on his clothes and make it clear that you will not spend more than that amount.
6. Get your child to agree that he will wear whatever clothing he selects until the clothes wear out or until he outgrows them.

Shopping for Clothes

When you take your child shopping: (Try to take only one child shopping at a time. In the long run, this will save you time and energy.)
1. Start out early in the morning so that your child will be refreshed and ready to work.
2. Take the clothing list with you.
3. Go to the stores that you have pre-selected.

4. Let your child select and try on garments of his choice. If he has a hard time choosing, select several garments and let him make his choices from your selections.

5. Avoid arguing with your child over petty issues such as color, print, style, etc. More important issues are cleaning requirements, fabric content, quality and durability of the garment, etc.

6. Purchase the garments your child chooses as long as they:

Meet the school requirements.

Are included on the clothing list.

Are compatible with your clothing budget.

And remember—your child's preference is the main criterion for the clothes you buy for him.

Organizing a Wardrobe

After you take your child shopping:

1. Help your child get rid of his worn-out or outgrown clothes before you put the new ones away. This is so that he won't have to dig through a pile of "old" clothes to get to the "good" ones.

2. Help your child organize his closets and drawers so that there are specific places for everything (including dirty clothes).

Try not to shop for your child more than two times a year. If you do, you'll end up spending more money than you need to. In addition, your child will have more clothes than is necessary. Generally speaking, I recommend that parents replenish their child's wardrobe in the fall (September) and again in the spring (March).

Of course, many children require a new pair of shoes as often as every three months. In addition, swimwear and sun clothes need to be purchased for the summer. But other than these things, shopping for clothes can realistically be limited to twice a year.

You may find the following chart helpful in deciding what your child's wardrobe should consist of. Of course, clothing needs vary from child to child, and no one clothing chart could be totally relevant to every situation. This particular chart is meant to serve only as a guideline.

I have not included a clothing chart for infants and toddlers since numerous books have wardrobe charts for this age. If you are unable to locate these books, consult the infant-toddler department of a good department store. They often have infant-toddler clothing charts available to the consumer.

CLOTHING FOR A SIX-MONTH PERIOD

Girl's

No.	Item
2	Nighties
1	Bathrobe
1	Bath slippers
7	Panties
1	Slip
7*	Socks
2**	Shoes
1	Boots
7***	Play outfits
2–3	Dress-up outfits
1	Warm coat (preferably with hood)
1	Raincoat
1	Lightweight jacket
1	Nice sweater
1	Snowsuit
1–2	Bathing suits

Boy's

No.	Item
2	Pajamas
1	Bathrobe
1	Bath slippers
7	Underwear
7*	Socks
2**	Shoes
1	Boots
5–7	T-shirts
4–5	Sturdy play pants
2–3	Dress-up outfits
1	Warm coat
1	Raincoat
1	Lightweight jacket or sweatshirt
1	Snowsuit
1–2	Bathing suits

* 5 for everyday, 2 for dress-up.
** 1 for play, the other for dress.
*** Pants and tops, jumpsuits, skirts and blouses, or dresses.

The numbers on the chart are based on the thought that most children wear an outfit once before it has to be washed, and the majority of American families wash on an average of once a week. If your children do not dirty clothes this rapidly or if you wash more frequently, your child may be able to get along with a much smaller wardrobe. Everything depends on you, your child and your family situation.

Now, before I leave the subject of clothing, a few more "words to the wise." You'll save a lot of wear and tear on your pocketbook and your nerves if you'll:

1. Buy all one kind and color of socks so that you won't end up with unmatched pairs.

2. Encourage your child to color-coordinate his entire wardrobe so that whatever items he pulls out of his closet or drawer will go together, if wearing things that "match" colorwise is important around your house.

3. Rotate your child's clothes. See that the clean clothes are put on the bottom of the stack and encourage your child to use the clothes on the top of the stack.

4. Bring your child in on planning his wardrobe as early as you can. Age two is a good time to start! Many of the ideas we've talked about in this section can be used with a two-year-old child.

5. Make sure to put your child's name on his clothes. A special kind of laundry tape and ink pen can be purchased for this purpose. Labeled clothing, jackets, boots, etc., usually end up in their owner's possession while unlabeled items end up in the Lost and Found!

SUMMARY

In regard to a child's clothing:

A. More important than how a child looks in an outfit is how he feels in it.

B. It is imperative that children help select their own clothes.

C. Children need to have a framework in which to function if they are to make wise choices regarding their wardrobes.
D. To provide this framework parents need to:
   1. Do research and make adequate preparations before taking a child shopping for clothes.
   2. Take the child shopping whenever clothes are being purchased for him.
   3. Get rid of old clothes and organize the new ones.
E. Parents should try to limit wardrobe shopping for their children to two times a year (spring and fall).
F. Parents should try to supply their children with an adequate amount of clothing.
G. A good wardrobe will provide children with:
   1. Socks that are mostly one color.
   2. Clothes that are color-coordinated.
   3. Clothes that the child has selected.
   4. Clothes that have the child's name written inside them.

CHILDREN'S POSSESSIONS (INCLUDING BOOKS, RECORDINGS, GAMES, TOYS, AND EQUIPMENT)

7. "Mine!"

Evenings around our house are usually pretty interesting. Bruce and I never know exactly what to expect from one moment to the next. Conversations range from "Who was Robin Hood?" to "Where do babies come from?"

One major source of these stimulating conversations is the printed and recorded material that our children have access to. Of course Christopher and Lisa have their favorites, but eventually every book, tape, and record within reach receives their attention.

It's all part of the game plan! I am fully aware of the fact that some subjects are more difficult to talk about than others. I am also aware that children respond better to conversations that originate with them. The old "Come, let's sit down and have a little talk" is not the best way to stimulate children to learn.

Bruce and I provide our children with a collection of books, tapes and records that includes everything from fantasy to science and nature. Then we get out of the way while the children look through the material that is provided, and the children decide which world they will explore next. After they have made the choice, then we make ourselves available to go through the material with them and answer any questions they may have.

We have had some marvelous things happen as a result. We attribute our success to the fact that children seem to be more receptive to subjects *they* have chosen to pursue.

If this approach to family education appeals to you, you may be interested in knowing how to set up a substantial book, tape, and record library for your child.

Don't hesitate because of money. Providing your child with good literature can be relatively inexpensive if you use your local library. Of course, you may want to purchase a few things for your child to keep—but you don't have to buy very much.

But before you go to the library or the bookstore, there are a few things you need to know.

Choosing Good Books, Tapes, and Records

First, what constitutes a good book, record or tape? Volumes have been written on this subject, but as far as I'm concerned, everything can be summed up in this one statement. *A good book, record or tape will be something that a child can understand, that will capture and retain his interest, and that will have a positive effect on his life.* The key here is "the positive effect on his life." We are well aware of the fact that a *Playboy* magazine may capture and retain a child's interest. The question is, will it have a positive effect on his life?

It should be noted at this point that the word "positive" is not necessarily synonymous with "educational." Some parents and educators feel that if something does not educate a child it is not positive. I would disagree. Things that appeal to a child's fantasy or stimulate his creativity are just as valuable as "educational material."

Over the last fifteen years, I've worked with a great deal of the vast amount of printed and recorded material now available for children. My experience has led me to believe that a good book, record, or tape will usually fall into one of six categories. (Of course, some books have the versatility that qualifies them for several categories.)

Awareness of these categories is especially important in order to make sure you expose your child to all of them. It is very easy to become so fascinated with one interest to the exclusion of all the rest. This is especially true of children if they are left on their own. It is unfortunate when this happens because every category has its own special contribution to add to a child's life. Thus I recommend that you help your child "expand" by giving him access to books, records, and tapes from all six of the following categories.

1. *Fantasy.* A sizeable portion of children's printed and recorded material falls into this category. These are the "just-for-fun" books, tapes, and records that stimulate a child's fantasy. These publications allow the child to remove himself from reality and delve into the world of make-believe. Needless to say, fantasy books and recordings are extremely valuable to the growth and development of a child's creativity and imagination. Included in this category are poetry and story books, records, and tapes.

2. *Technique.* Technique books, records, and tapes show or tell children how to do things. They may teach a child how to dance or offer guidelines for making a puppet. Detailed instructions are usually included. These publications are good for developing art, craft, musical, and physical skills. They also enhance a child's ability to assimilate and follow directions. Included in this category are materials about cooking, carpentry, sewing, arts and crafts, magic, music, dance,

rhythm and body movement, physical skills, drama, puppets, costuming, toy-making, etc.

3. *Participation.* Books and recordings in this category cause children to say or do something. Materials in this category ask questions that need to be answered, have pictures that need to be completed, provide puzzles that need to be solved, etc. These publications are commonly called "activity" books, records or tapes and are especially valuable because of their ability to move children from passive involvement to active involvement. Included in this category are riddle, maze, question and answer, optical illusion, and sensory experience books, records, and tapes.

4. *Academic.* These books, records, and tapes deal with subjects such as reading, writing, arithmetic, social studies, science and nature, etc. These publications provide the information necessary for a child's academic education. Included in this category are resource materials such as encyclopedias, dictionaries, text books, and other references that provide factual information. Sex education materials are also included in this category.

5. *Affirmational.* These books and recordings affirm children. They help a child discover who he is and they tell him that he is okay. These materials develop a child's understanding and appreciation of himself and the people around him. Included in this category are materials that deal with feelings, needs, rights, and personal problems (such as wearing glasses, hearing aids, or braces; bed-wetting, thumb-sucking, etc.) Trauma education materials are also included in this category.

6. *Inspirational and Religious.* Books, records, and tapes in this category inspire children into self-actualization and positive social encounters. They motivate children to "become" and "give of themselves" in a healthy way. Needless to say, these materials contribute greatly to developing a positive self-concept and good social skills. Included in this

category are fiction and non-fiction, poetry and story books, records and tapes.

The Positive Effects of Using Good Books, Tapes, and Records

A combination of books, records and tapes from all six of these categories will:

1. *Help your child develop a positive self-concept.* This will happen as your child learns that he is similar to other human beings and yet unique in his own way. Good printed material will also bring him in touch with his basic human rights, emotions, and needs.

2. *Help your child develop good social skills.* This will occur as he is exposed, through quality books, records, and tapes, to communication skills and to the various facets of interpersonal relationships.

3. *Stimulate your child's intellectual growth and development.* Good publications will provide your child with accurate information that he can relate to. In addition, good books, records, and tapes will motivate him to ask questions and explore.

4. *Assist your child in making decisions and solving problems.* As your child observes other people making wise decisions and coming up with good solutions, he will learn to do the same. Good books, records, and tapes give children an opportunity to observe other people while they make decisions and solve problems.

5. *Assist in developing your child's ethics and values.* Good printed and recorded material can support and reinforce the ethics and values that a child is being taught at home, at church, and at school.

6. *Help prepare your child for the future.* Appropriate materials can help parents and teachers expose children to the future and prepare them to cope with it.

All of this is to say that good books, records, and tapes are an essential part of the program. It may take some work to get the appropriate materials together, but your efforts will really pay off. And who knows, you might even learn something in the process. If it weren't for my son's book about dinosaurs, I may have lived my entire life without knowing what a Brachiosaurus is!

Every day, all over the world, children cry out, "There's nothing to do!" For every cry, there's an exasperated parent responding, "You have more than I ever thought of having! And yet you are bored! Why?"

The answer is simple. A child can have access to a million toys, but if the toys aren't the right kind or if they aren't presented in the right way, they will be meaningless. We're going to talk about how you can get the "right kind" of game, toy, or piece of equipment and present it in the right way, but first, allow me to start at the beginning.

While gathering the data for this chapter, I became extremely fascinated with children's playthings. I wanted to learn more about them than I was able to get from books, so I began seeking out new experiences. Finally, I came up with a brilliant idea! Why not work in a toy store? I applied for a job at the San Marino Toy Shoppe and was hired to sell toys during the Christmas holidays. What an education I got!

To begin with, I discovered first hand what motivates parents to purchase the things they do for their children. Generally speaking, many parents buy a game, toy or piece of equipment for their child because of:

Personal preference (the parent likes the toy and in some way wishes he had one).

The appearance of the toy (the parent likes the looks of a toy and thinks that it is "cute" or "darling" or "beautiful").

Nostalgia (the toy is similar to one the parent loved and enjoyed as a child or it reminds him of a special time, place or person).

The educational value of the toy (despite its "play"

value, parents like the toy because it will teach their child something).

The functional value of the toy (the toy will accomplish a specific purpose; parents like things that "mean" something or will "do" something).

The toy fascinates the parent (the parent finds the toy provocative and is interested in how it is put together or what it is able to do).

These are not necessarily wrong reasons for buying a toy. But if one or all of these reasons is the *only* criterion for selecting a toy, parents run the risk of buying a "miss" instead of a "hit." *Toys that are bought should meet the needs and desires of the child rather than the needs and desires of the parent.*

It is true that many parents aren't making it when it comes to buying toys for their children, but this is not to say that children should be left to make their own selections without parental guidance. My experience at the toy store taught me that children usually buy:

The toys they see on TV.

The toys their friends have.

The toys that look good on the shelf in the store.

The toys that they can afford (if a child has money to spend, he will often spend it on anything just to be spending it!).

No wonder toys end up in the trash can or gathering dust on the shelf!

Choosing Good Games, Toys, and Equipment

Both parents and children need to have better reasons for buying the things they do.

The following are good criteria for selecting games, toys, and equipment:

1. *Versatility.* The things that are provided for children should have more than one use. This not only promotes

creative thinking, but also insures that the article will be used more than one time. Nothing is worse than buying a toy for a child and having it discarded after using it only once.

2. *Durability.* Anything a child uses receives a "workout." Avoid disappointments and upsets by providing things that do not break easily.

3. *Workability.* Nothing is more frustrating than something that does not work either because it is broken or because it is "fake." Plastic hammers that do not hammer and plastic lipstick that is not real are frustrating. Make sure that toys and equipment are in good repair and that they do what they are supposed to do.

4. *Suitability for independent play.* Do not provide things for children that require a lot of adult supervision to use. The more that children do on their own, the more valid their experiences will be. Make sure to provide children with things they are physically and mentally ready to handle. If you give them things that are beyond their abilities, they are likely to fail.

5. *Attractiveness.* Remember to provide things that are attractive to the child. If a child really wants a toy, he will appreciate and use it more. If he is not attracted to the object, it is unlikely that he will use it.

6. *Safety.* For your peace of mind and your child's safety, make sure that he is surrounded with safe toys and equipment. Check each item you buy to see that it does not have:

    sharp points
    sharp edges
    small parts that could be swallowed by a young child
    pinch points (springs, hinges, etc.)
    shear points

Also try to get things that are:

    cleanable
    non-allergenic
    non-flammable
    non-toxic

Make sure to avoid toys made of glass and brittle plastic, and do not have infant toys with cords more than twelve inches long.

Also, make sure that there is a variety of things for your child to do and that some of those things encourage him to play with other children. Some toys are designed to be shared. A few of these are good to have.

Just as books, records, and tapes have categories, so do games, toys, and equipment. Again, it is wise to expose children to items from each category in order to broaden their experience and help them grow and develop.

Here is a list of the game, toy, and equipment categories.

1. *Role Playing*. Role-playing toys, games, and equipment allow a child to temporarily become someone or something other than who he really is. These items encourage healthy imitation and identification. They allow a child to put himself into the role of another person, animal or object. Role-playing toys, games, and equipment are invaluable to a child's mental, social, and emotional growth.

Among the items in this category are:

    animal sets
    cash register
    circus sets
    costumes
    doctor kits
    dolls and doll accessories; doll house and furniture
    hats
    "hero" sets (cowboy, space man, etc.)
    housekeeping equipment
    make-up
    miniature transportation toys
    nurse kits
    paper dolls
    puppets
    structures that could be converted into play house, store, theater, garage, etc.

2. *Building and Construction.* Building and construction playthings offer the child small parts or components that he can put together to construct a "whole." Many of these items have interlocking pieces; others snap together or screw into each other. Stacking and nesting toys also fit into this category. Items in this group develop creativity, abstract thinking, and problem-solving. They also increase a child's awareness and understanding of spatial relationships.

Included in this category are:

beads
blocks
Bristle Blocks
carpentry tools and supplies
cartons or wooden boxes
Click
Connect-a-Cube
Crystal Climbers
Design blocks
Erector sets
Fischer Technik
flannel board
Girdle and Panel
Leg-o
Lincoln Logs
mallet and wooden pegs
Meccano
nuts and bolts
peg boards
puzzles
Tinker Toys
wooden pegs
wooden planks

3. *Art and Crafts.* Art and craft materials and supplies give children opportunities to communicate in nonverbal ways. They develop craftsmanship and contribute to the development of a child's creativity.

Included in this category are:
- basket weaving materials
- beadwork materials
- chalk and chalkboard
- collage materials
- colored chalk
- colored construction paper
- craft sticks
- crayons
- Etch-a-sketch
- fingerpaints
- glue
- gummed paper
- hobby sets
- jewelry making materials
- leather
- metal craft sets
- models
- modeling compounds
- origami materials
- paints
- paintbrushes
- paste
- plain paper
- plastic
- scissors
- sewing and stitchery equipment and materials
- spirograph
- watercolor pens
- weaving materials and supplies
- wood
- wood-burning sets

4. *Exploration and Discovery*. These items stimulate a child's thinking process and motivate him to learn. They facilitate children in making discoveries that contribute to their awareness and understanding of the world around them.

These games, toys and equipment are very important to the intellectual growth and development of a child.

Included in this category are:
batteries
binoculars
camera
chemistry sets
compass
crib mobiles
electric bell switch
electric cord
flashlight
gyroscope
magic set
magnets
magnifying glass
microscope
pets
prisms
sand toys
science kits
stethoscope
sun dial
telescope
thermometer
wading pool
water toys

5. *Academic.* Games, toys, and equipment in this category teach and reinforce academic facts and concepts. Included in this category are:
abacus
alphabet blocks
alphabet sets
anagrams
barometer
categorization items

checkers
chess
clocks
dominoes
films
film strips
flash cards
globes
Lotto
maps
meter stick
micrometer
models of geometric figures
number games
number line
Parchesi
play money
printing sets
protractor
slides
speedometer
tape measure
three-minute timer
typewriter
Viewmaster
weighing scales

6. *Physical Skills*. These games, toys, and equipment help children develop their muscles. They also develop a child's muscular coordination and equip him with various physical skills.

Included in this category are:
ball and ten pins
bars
baton
bean bags
bikes

climbing toys
dodge ball
equipment for:
   badminton
   baseball
   basketball
   camping
   croquet
   fishing
   football
   golf
   hockey
   shuffleboard
   soccer
   ping pong
   tennis
finger tops
Frisbee
garden tools (including rakes and shovels)
hoops
jump rope
kites
ladders
marbles
miscellaneous balls
miscellaneous wheel toys
paddle and ball
pogo sticks
pull toys
punching bag
push toys
rings
ring toss
rocking chair
rocking horse
ropes

    scooters
    skates
    sled
    stick horse
    stilts
    swimming pool
    swings
    tether ball
    threading block
    trikes
    tumbling mat
    wagons
    yo-yo

    7. *Music and Rhythm.* Items in this category contribute to a child's awareness and appreciation of music. They often teach a child musical concepts and enable him to play musical instruments and dance. In addition, they teach him sound discrimination.

    Included in this category are:
    autoharp
    bells
    blocks and scrapers
    chimes
    harmonica
    jew's harp
    kazoo
    marimba
    melody bells
    miscellaneous brass instruments (trumpet, trombone, tuba, etc.)
    miscellaneous percussion instruments (drums, cymbals, castanets, etc.)
    miscellaneous stringed instruments (violin, viola, cello, string bass, guitar, etc.)
    miscellaneous woodwind instruments (flute, clarinet, saxophone, etc.)

music boxes
musical tops
radio
recorder
record player and records
rhythm sticks
shakers and sound rattles
tape recorder
triangles
whistles
xylophone

8. *Novelty*. These items are the "just for fun" games, toys and equipment that have no special meaning or purpose. They are often entertaining and are purchased for the sole purpose of enjoyment. Although I do not recommend giving children lots of novelty items, one every so often can be fun. It should be noted, however, that these things do not always last a long time, nor do they retain a child's interest.

Included in this category are:

battery-operated toys
gags
gimmicks
interesting visual toys
kaleidoscopes
octascopes
periscopes
trinkets
wind-up toys

Properly Presenting Games, Toys, and Equipment

So far we've talked about selecting the right things. Now it is time to talk about presenting them in the right way.

When providing things for your children, do not give them everything at once. Remember that the effectiveness or "life" of a toy is approximately one month. If a toy is always there it becomes a dead toy. This is one of the reasons children often say "there's nothing to do" even though their closets are packed full of toys.   A limited number of toys should be made available every month and the rest put away. At the beginning of each month a new group of toys is brought out and the old group is put away. The lives of the new toys have been renewed, and it's almost like Christmas for the child.

Toy rotation will work until the child completely outgrows a toy. When this happens, the toy should be disposed of. Nothing is more frustrating to a parent and a child than a closet full of dead or outgrown toys.

Another thing that parents need to reevaluate is the time at which a child receives toys. Most parents depend on Christmas and birthdays to provide a child with all of the toys he is to own. The unfortunate thing about this tradition is that the child receives everything at once and everything dies at the same time. It would be far more effective if parents would cut down on Christmas and birthdays and spread their giving out over the year. Less could be given on Christmas and birthdays and small gifts could be provided on other holidays or special occasions.

Owning Things

Whether we're talking about books, records, tapes, toys, games, or equipment, children have a right to own their own things.

Items that are given to a child or ones that he acquires on his own belong to him. This means that as long as he does not hurt himself or others, he should have control over his possessions. He should be allowed to decide whether or not he will share his things and he should be allowed to determine how his things will be used.

Of course parents should discourage children from abusing or misusing their things. The best way to do this is for parents to refuse to replace the things a child has lost, damaged, or broken. If abused or misused items need to be repaired or replaced, it should be the responsibility of the child to do so.

"But what if someone else breaks a child's toy?" No matter! The child who owns something is ultimately responsible for it. Whatever happens to his possessions is his responsibility. If he does not want his things lost, misused, damaged, or destroyed, he needs to see that:

1. They are put away when they are not being used.
2. They are not loaned to anyone who may abuse them.

If a child has outgrown a possession or if he has decided that he no longer wants to keep it, he should be able to decide how he is going to get rid of it. In order to make a wise decision, a child needs to know what all of his options are. They are as follows:

A child can get rid of a possession that he no longer wants by:

>Putting it away and saving it as a memento from his childhood.

>Giving it to someone else who wants or needs it.

>Trading it for something that he wants.

>Selling it.

All of this is to say that the next time your child clutches onto a possession and screams "Mine!" make sure that both you and he fully understand and accept exactly what he is saying!

SUMMARY

In regard to children's books, records and tapes:
A. The criteria for a good book, record, or tape are:
   1. It should be something that a child can understand.
   2. It should capture and retain a child's interest.
   3. It should have a positive effect on a child's life.

B. Good books, records or tapes usually fall into one of the
    following categories:
    1. Fantasy.
    2. Technique.
    3. Participation.
    4. Academic.
    5. Affirmational.
    6. Inspirational and Religious.
C. Parents should try to expose children to publications from
    all six categories.
D. Good books, records, and tapes will:
    1. Help a child develop a positive self-concept.
    2. Help a child develop good social skills.
    3. Stimulate a child's intellectual growth and development.
    4. Assist a child in making decisions and solving prob-
       lems.
    5. Assist in developing a child's ethics and values.
    6. Help prepare a child for the future.

In regard to games, toys and equipment:
A. Toys that are bought should meet the needs and desires of
    the child rather than the needs and desires of the parent.
B. In selecting games, toys, and equipment, keep in mind
    that an item should:
    1. Be versatile.
    2. Be durable.
    3. Work properly.
    4. Promote independence.
    5. Be attractive.
    6. Be safe.
C. Good games, toys, and equipment should also promote a
    certain amount of social interaction.
D. Good games, toys, and equipment usually fall into one of
    the following categories:
    1. Role playing.
    2. Building and constructing.

  3. Arts and crafts.
  4. Exploration and discovery.
  5. Academic.
  6. Physical skill.
  7. Music and rhythms.
  8. Novelty.
E. Parents should try to expose children to items from all
   eight categories.
F. For maximum use, games, toys, and equipment should be:
  1. Rotated.
  2. Given to children throughout the year instead of twice
     a year.

In regard to owning things:
A. Children need to own and be responsible for their own
   things.
B. A child should be allowed to decide how he is going to
   get rid of a possession that he has outgrown or no longer
   wants to keep.

BOOKS FOR CHAPTER SEVEN

Good books for parents to read regarding the things
mentioned in this chapter are:
Growing Up with Toys, Irene Clepper. Minneapolis: Augs-
   burg Publishing House, 1974.
Play: Children's Business. Washington, D.C.: Association for
   Childhood Education International, 1976.
*Selecting Educational Equipment and Materials for School
   and Home.* Washington, D.C.: Association for Childhood Education International, 1976.
Good books for children to read regarding the things
mentioned in this chapter:

Arts and Crafts

Arts and Crafts You Can Eat, Viccki Cobb. Philadelphia:
J. B. Lippincott Co., 1974.

Art Recipes, Doris E. Foley. Dansville, N.Y.: The Instructor
Publications, Inc., 1966.

Craft Fun: Easy to Do Projects with Simple Materials, Janet
R. McCarty and Betty J. Peterson. New York: Golden
Press, 1975.

Creating with Paper, Pauline Johnson. Seattle: University of
Washington Press, 1975.

Exciting Things to Do with Color, Janet Allen. Philadelphia
and New York: J. B. Lippincott Co., 1977.

Exciting Things to Do with Nature Materials, Judy Allen.
Philadelphia and New York: J. B. Lippincott Co., 1977.

Exciting Things to Make with Paper, Ruth Thomson. Philadelphia and New York: J. B. Lippincott Co., 1977.

Exciting Things to Make with Wool, String and Thread,
Rosalind May and Sheila Brull. Philadelphia and New
York: J. B. Lippincott Co., 1977.

Felt Craft, Florence Temko. Garden City, New York:
Doubleday, 1973.

Flying Origami, Eiji Nakamura. Tokyo: Japan Publications,
1972.

Fold, Paste, Whittle, Paint and Hammer, Robert Pierce. New
York: Golden Press, 1974.

*Ginny Graves' Discovery Stuff: Twelve Months of Creative
Art Ideas,* Ginny Graves. Shawnee Mission, Kansas:
Discovery Stuff, 1977.

Introducing Crayon Techniques, Henry Pluckrose. New York:
Watson-Guptill Publications, 1972.

Jewelry Making, Paul Villiard. Garden City, New York:
Doubleday, 1973.

Let's Build, Rita Davies. New York: Van Nostrand Reinhold Co., 1974.

Let's Decorate Fabric, Elizabeth Holder. New York: Van Nostrand Reinhold Co., 1974.

Let's Paint, Rita Davies. New York: Van Nostrand Reinhold Co., 1971.

Making Things: The Hand Book of Creative Discovery. Ann Wiseman. Boston: Little, Brown and Co.

Making Things II: A Hand Book of Creative Discovery. Ann Wiseman. Boston: Little, Brown and Co.

Paper Cutting, Florence Temko. Garden City, N.Y.: Doubleday, 1973.

Pholdit, S. Goldberg. Billiken Publications, Inc., 1972.

Printmaking, Harlow Rockwell. Garden City, N.Y.: Doubleday, 1973.

Recipes for Art and Craft Materials, Helen Roney Sattler. New York: Lothrop, Lee & Shepard Co., 1973.

Sheet Magic: Games, Toys and Gifts from Old Sheets, Peggy Parish. New York: The Macmillan Co., 1971.

Snips and Snails and Walnut Whales: Nature Crafts for Children, Phyllis Fiarotta. New York: Workman Publishing Co., 1975.

Sticks and Stones and Ice Cream Cones, Phyllis Fiarotta. New York: Workman Publishing Co., 1973.

String Art, Lois Kreischer. New York: Crown Publishers Inc., 1971.

String Projects, Helen Jill Fletcher. Garden City, N.Y.: Doubleday, 1974.

Superbook of Things to Make, Pia Hsiao and Neil Lorimer. New York: Platt & Munk Publishers, 1976.

Touch, Joy Wilt and Terre Watson. Waco, Texas: Educational Products Division, Word, Inc., 1977.

The You and Me Heritage Tree: Ethnic Crafts for Children, Phyllis Fiarotta and Noel Fiarotta. New York: Workman Publishing Co., 1976.

Carpentry

Carpentry for Children, Jerome E. Leavitt. New York: Sterling Publishing Co., Inc., 1973.

Carpentry: Making Things with Wood. McPhee Gribble Publishers, Penguin Books Australia Ltd., 1976.

Fun with Wood, Mark Harwood. New York: Grosset & Dunlap, 1975.

Woodworking Projects for Elementary Grades, C. J. Maginley. Darien, Conn.: Teachers Publishing Corp., 1967.

Costumes

Be What You Want to Be! The Complete Dressup and Pretend Craft Book, Phyllis Fiarotta and Noel Fiarotta. New York: Workman Publishing Co., 1977.

Costumes to Make, Peggy Parish. New York: Macmillan Publishing Co., Inc., 1970.

Easy Costumes You Don't Have To Sew, Goldie Taub Chernoff. New York: Scholastic Book Services, 1975.

The Great Pretenders, Joy Wilt and Kathy Berry. Waco, Tex.: Educational Products Division, Word, Inc., 1977.

Lots of Fun to Dress Up, Colette Lamarque. London: Collins, 1973.

Making Costumes for Parties, Plays and Holidays, Alice Gilbreath. New York: William Morrow and Co., 1974.

The Little Witch's Black Magic Book of Disguises, Linda Glovach. Englewood Cliffs, N.J.: Prentice-Hall, Inc., 1973.

More Great Pretenders, Joy Wilt and Kathy Berry. Waco, Tex.: Educational Products Division, Word, Inc., 1977.

Equipment

Handcrafted Playgrounds: Designs You Can Build Yourself, M. Paul Friedberg. New York: Random House, 1975.

Handmade Secret Hiding Places, Nonny Hogrogian. Woodstock, N.Y.: The Overlook Press, 1975.

Housebuilding for Children, Les Walker. Woodstock, N.Y.: The Overlook Press, 1977.

Making Children's Furniture and Play Structures, Bruce Palmer. New York: Workman Publishing Co., 1974.

Play Structures, Gail Ellison. Pasadena, Calif.: Pacific Oaks College, 1974.

Wheels, Boxes and Skateboards, William Jaber. New York: Drake Publishers, Inc., 1977.

Workyards, Nancy Rudolph. New York: Teachers College Press, 1974.

Games

Anytime, Anywhere, Anybody Games, Andrea DiNoto. New York: Golden Press, 1977.

Backyard Games, Eric Lincoln. New York: Stadia Sports Publishing, Inc., 1973.

Bike, Skate and Skateboard Games, Michael Donner. New York: Golden Press, 1977.

Creating and Using Learning Games, Craig Pearson and Joseph Marfuggi. Palo Alto, Calif.: Learning Handbooks, 1975.

Everybody's a Winner, Tom Schneider. Boston: Little, Brown & Co., 1976.

The Fun and Games Book: Starring Donald the Dinosaur, Barbara Kruger Bate. New York: Platt & Munk, 1967.

The Fun and Games Book: Starring Leon the Lion, Barbara Kruger Bate, New York: Platt & Munk, 1967.

Games and Puzzles You Can Make Yourself, Harvey Weiss. New York: Thomas Y. Crowell Co., 1976.

Game Things, Joy Wilt and Gwen Hurn. Waco, Tex.: Educational Products Division, Word, Inc., 1978.

Games to Make and Play, Brian Edwards. Chicago: Rand McNally & Co., 1974.

Jump Rope! Peter L. Skolnik. New York: Workman Publishing Co., 1974.

The Great American Book of Sidewalk, Stoop, Dirt, Curb and Alley Games, Fred Ferretti. New York: Workman Publishing Co., 1975.

The Great American Marble Book, Fred Ferretti. New York: Workman Publishing Co., 1973.

The Know How Book of Action Games, Anne Civardi. New York: Sterling Publishing Co., 1976.

The New Games Book. Garden City, N.Y.: Doubleday & Co., 1976.

The World Book of Children's Games, Arnold Arnold. Greenwich, Conn.: Fawcett Crest, 1972.

Musical Instruments

Ball, Rope, Hoop Activities, Jack J. Capon. Belmont, Calif.: Fearon Publishers Inc., 1975.

Listen! Joy Wilt and Terre Watson, Waco, Tex.: Educational Products Division, Word, Inc., 1977.

Lively Craft Cards: Make Your Own Musical Instrument, Peter Williams. New York: World Publishing Co., 1972.

Make Your Own Musical Instruments, Muriel Mandell and Robert E. Wood. New York: Sterling Publishing Co., Inc., 1971.

Making Music Around the Home and Yard, Emil and Celeste Richards. New York: Award Music Co., 1974.

Making Music in Mommy's Kitchen, Emil and Celeste Richards. New York: Award Music Co., 1974.

Rhythm and Movement, Joy Wilt and Terre Watson. Waco, Tex.: Educational Products Division, Word, Inc., 1977.

Whistles and Strings. New York: McGraw-Hill Book Co., 1971.

Puppets

Fun with Puppets, Vera Brody and Marie Francoise Heron. New York: Franklin Watts, Inc., 1975.

More Puppets with Pizazz, Joy Wilt, Gwen Hurn and John Hurn. Waco, Tex.: Educational Products Division, Word, Inc., 1977.

Puppets for All Grades, Louise Binder Scott, Marion E. May and Mildred S. Shaw. Dansville, N.Y.: F. A. Owen Publishing Co., 1960.

Puppet Party, Goldie Taub Chernoff. New York: Walker & Co., 1971.

Puppet People. The Danbury Press, 1972.

Puppet Stages and Props with Pizazz, Joy Wilt, Gwen Hurn, and John Hurn. Waco, Tex.: Educational Products Division, Word, Inc., 1977.

Puppets with Pizazz, Joy Wilt, Gwen Hurn, and John Hurn. Waco, Tex.: Educational Products Division, Word, Inc., 1977.

Toys

American Folk Toys: How to Make Them, Dick Schnacke. Baltimore: Penguin Books, Inc., 1973.

The Boomerang Book, M. J. Hanson. Great Britain: Puffin Books, 1974.

Boomerangs, How to Make and Throw Them, Bernard S. Mason. New York: Dover Publications, Inc., 1974.

Folding Paper Toys, Shari Lewis and Lillian Oppenheimer. New York: Stein and Day, 1963.

Folk Toys Around the World and How to Make Them, John Joseph. New York: Parents' Magazine Press, 1972.

Go Fly a Kite, Ray Brock. Lenox, Mass.: Hawthorne Press, 1976.

The Great International Paper Airplane Book, Jerry Mander, George Dippel and Howard Gossage. New York: Simon and Schuster, 1967.

How to Make Snop Snappers and Other Fine Things, Robert Lopshire. New York: Greenwillow Books, 1977.

How to Make Wooden Toys and Games, Walter E. Schutz. New York: Collier Books, 1975.

The Mickey Mouse Make-It Book. New York: Random House, 1974.

Play Book, Steven Caney. New York: Workman Publishing Co., 1975.

Professor Hammerfinger's Indestructible Toys, Steve Ross. Willits, Calif.: Oliver Press, 1975.

Things to Make: Fun Stuff You Can Make All By Yourself, Robert Lopshire. New York: Random House, 1964.

Toy Book, Steven Caney. New York: Workman Publishing Co., 1972.

Toys to Make, Brian Edwards. Chicago: Rand McNally & Co., 1974.

Trash Can Toys and Games, Leonard Todd. Dallas, Pa.: Penguin Books, 1974.

Twenty-Five Kites That Fly, Leslie L. Hunt. New York: Dover Publications, Inc., 1971.

Miscellaneous

Do a Zoom Do, Bernice Chesler, editor. Boston: Little, Brown & Co., 1975.

The Everything Book, Eleanor Graham Vance. New York: Golden Press, 1974.

The Great Perpetual Learning Machine, Jim Blake and Barbara Ernst. Boston: Little, Brown & Co., 1976.

I Saw a Purple Cow and 100 Other Recipes for Learning, Ann Cole, Carolyn Haas, Faith Bushness, and Betty Weinberger. Boston: Little, Brown and Co., 1972.

Just a Box? Goldie Taub Chernoff. New York: Walker & Co., 1973.

The Kids' Kitchen Takeover, Sara Bennett Stein. New York: Workman Publishing Co., 1975.

Look! Joy Wilt and Terre Watson, Waco, Tex.: Educational Products Division, Word, Inc., 1978.

Recyclopedia: Games, Science Equipment and Crafts from Recycled Materials, Robin Simons. Boston: Houghton Mifflin Co., 1976.

The Second Whole Kids Catalog, Peter Cardozo. New York: Bantam Books, 1977.

The Whole Kids Catalog, Peter Cardozo. New York: Bantam Books, 1975.

Workjobs, Mary Baratta-Lorton. Menlo Park, Calif.: Addison-Wesley Publishing Co., 1972.

8. "2-4-6-8, Johnny Caught a Rattlesnake!"

"P.U.!" Christopher gasped as he rolled out of bed one Saturday morning. By this time the pungent smell that had awakened Bruce and me at 3:00 A.M. had permeated the whole house. A family of skunks had sought shelter from the rain that had poured down the night before. Unfortunately, they found the warm, dry area under our house to be most satisfactory.

"What's that smell?" Lisa asked as she joined the rest of the family in the kitchen. "Skunks!" I moaned. "Oh, goodie!" she shrieked. "Can we keep them?" "Absolutely not!" I snapped. Lisa began to cry. "But I want a skunk," she protested. "I'll call it 'Flower' just like in Bambi." *

That did it! As though I didn't have enough problems on my hands with a family of skunks living under our house, now I was facing the decision of whether or not I was going to

---

* Ownership of skunks is illegal in many states because they are top candidates for carrying rabies. Caution is advised.

deprive my child of the enriching experience of owning a skunk. "Look, Lisa," I screamed, "this isn't Bambi's forest and life isn't a Walt Disney movie!"

Truer words were never spoken—but you'd never know it by the responses I got when I asked a group of children, "What would you choose if you could have any pet you wanted?"

"A fox like Robin Hood!"

"A bear like Gentle Ben!"

"A shaggy dog like the one in *The Shaggy D.A.!*"

"Black Beauty!"

"A bird like Baretta's!"

. . . And so on.

Could these children possibly understand the meaning of their choices? Not really.

Unlike these kids, you and I know that real foxes don't wear green Robin Hood suits, most bears aren't all that gentle, the shaggy dog's hair gets matted if it isn't combed frequently, Black Beauty probably got cranky if he wasn't exercised constantly, and even Baretta's bird dirties his cage!

No, there's no way a child could fully understand why his mother faints dead away when, after a trip to the zoo, the child announces nonchalantly, "I'm saving up my allowance to buy a boa constrictor!"

A lot of the information children receive about pets via TV, movies, books, etc., is unrealistic. (So what's new?) Unfortunately, in this particular con job the animals, who don't watch TV, go to the movies or read books, are unfairly dragged into the whole mess, and they have more at stake in the human-pet relationship than the humans do. Many pets end up neglected, abused, and even killed.

Before going any further, I think it's only fair to tell you where I stand in regard to animal life in general (just in case you haven't read between the lines in this chapter so far). I'm the type who will spend fifteen minutes capturing a spider in a paper cup so that I can transport it outside rather than killing it. I respect life—anyone's or anything's—and I try to transfer this respect to my children.

This is exactly why my home is not a menagerie of pets. Pets are not toys! They need *consistent* tender loving care. Granted, most children have a lot of love to give, and I'm not trying to deny this fact. The thing that worries me is the consistency with which it is administered. Inconsistency is a normal trait of childhood. Most children have a great deal of difficulty doing anything every day or all the time. Pet care is an every day, all-the-time thing. Very few pets require "little or no care."

"But," you may say, "isn't it good for children to have pets?" Let's talk about this.

It is true that animals make great companions. They are also entertaining and educational, but the animal neglect and abuse that often results from children owning pets isn't good for anyone. It obviously isn't good for the animal, and it isn't good for the child. I've known a lot of kids to have a great deal of guilt over maiming or killing an animal.

Thus, the decision whether or not a child should own a pet is a big and important one. So the next time your child begs to have one of the neighbors' thirteen kittens, there are several things you should consider before you say "yes."

Qualifications for Pet Owners

If you've got a child who gets a kick out of kicking dogs, pulling cats' tails, picking the legs off of spiders, or pouring salt on snails, it's obvious he doesn't have a basic love and respect for living things. In this case you'd better think twice before you allow him to own a pet. If, on the other hand, your child loves and respects living things, he meets the number one qualification for pet owners.

But love and respect are not enough. A child needs to understand living things before he can own one. He needs to realize that an animal's life is dependent upon many factors. A

lack in this area may mean that your child will not take seriously his responsibility for sustaining and enhancing the life of
his pet.

All too often "wanting" a pet is the only thing that warrants
getting one. This is important, of course, but it's only the
beginning. Whenever a child asks to have a pet, the parents
need to ask:

1. Does my child love, respect, and understand living
   things?
2. Is my child willing and able to give his pet the care that
   it needs?
3. Does my child understand the commitment involved in
   owning a pet?

A "yes" answer to all of these questions says that your
child has the potential to be a responsible pet owner.

Choosing a Pet

Several summers ago, a veterinarian and I teamed up to
teach a class called "Critter Care." The class dealt with
choosing, obtaining, and caring for pets. Any child who was
in the process of choosing a pet was required to do some research before making his choice. We gave him a list of questions and we stressed the importance of going to more than
one source for his answers. We referred him to:

The library
The zoo
Nature centers
Animal welfare organizations like the Humane Society
Pet stores
A veterinarian
Pet owners

Some children did their research in person, others did it
over the telephone or by mail. These are the questions they
were required to find answers for:

ALL ABOUT _____
(NAME OF THE ANIMAL)

LIFE SPAN:

How long is the animal supposed to live?

_____

LIVING CONDITIONS:

Should this animal be kept indoors or outdoors?

_____

Should this animal be kept where it is warm or cold?

_____

What kind of house or shelter, if any, does this animal need (cage, vivarium, aquarium, serpentarium, hutch, shed, coop, pen, fenced-in yard, etc.)?

_____

DIET:

What does this animal eat?

_____

HABITS:

Does this animal like and respond positively to human beings?

_____

When and for how long does this animal sleep?

_____

When is this animal most active?

_____

CARE:

How often does this animal need to be fed?

_____

How often does this animal need to be watered?

_____

How often does this animal's home need to be cleaned?

_____

What cleaning and grooming does this animal need?

_____

Does this animal need to be trained? _____

Does this animal need to be exercised? _____

 If so, how often? _____

Does this animal need immunizations (shots)? _____

 If so, what are they? _____

List other special requirements this animal may have.

_____

_____

ILLNESS (SICKNESS):

What are common illnesses for this pet?

_____

_____

How can they be avoided?

_____

What will help cure these illnesses?

_____

COST:

How much will this animal cost to buy? _____

How much will the home and equipment for this animal cost?

_____

How much will it cost to feed and take care of this animal?

_____

SPECIAL PROBLEMS:

What special problems would owning this animal cause?

_____

_____

It never failed! Every time we handed this questionnaire to a child, it was received with moans and groans. "Gee whiz," one boy complained, "this is worse than homework!"

"Yeah!" my veterinarian friend responded. "But if you don't have enough of what it takes to get the answers to these questions, you probably won't have what it takes to care for a pet!"

I agreed wholeheartedly. If a child isn't willing to find out about a pet before he gets it, chances are he won't take care of it after he has it.

"But won't this research paper discourage children from having pets?" a concerned pet advocate asked.

"Probably," my co-teacher answered, "and that's good!

Children need to know exactly what they're getting into before they take on a pet!"

Many children in the class decided against having certain pets after they discovered what was involved in owning and caring for them. We felt this was good.

The children who made it past the research had two more hurdles to go before they actually purchased their pets. Their next assignment was to fill out this questionnaire.

NAME _____

DATE _____

NAME OF ANIMAL _____

YES	NO	
____	____	I have asked my family for permission to own this animal.
____	____	I have made sure that no one in my family is allergic to or terrified by this animal.
____	____	No one in my family will be bothered by the habits of this animal.
____	____	My family and I are aware of the special problems having this animal may cause.
____	____	I can provide adequate living conditions for this animal.
____	____	I can provide an adequate diet for this animal.
____	____	I am willing and able to provide adequate care for this animal.
____	____	I am willing to do everything I can to help this animal if he gets injured or sick.
____	____	I can afford to purchase this animal anything that he needs to live a normal, healthy life.

We suggested that a "no" answer to any question on the questionnaire should cause a child to reconsider getting the animal.

"But what about young children who cannot do the research and fill out the questionnaire?" a mother once asked. "The parents will have to assume the responsibility for the pet," I answered. "But *I* don't want the pet!" she protested. "My *daughter* does!"

How many times has a parent given in to a child's pleas for a pet only to find that the child soon loses interest in the pet and the parent ends up owning and caring for it? I'm afraid that I'd have to "join the crowd" on this one. I continually wind up in a situation where I'm saying to myself, "When did I ever ask for something else to take care of?" (As though two kids weren't enough!)

Like the time Lisa decided that she just couldn't live without a mouse. Then she decided that her mouse just couldn't live without a companion. Of course, the two darling mice she chose were too small for us to determine their sex, and so— you guessed it! We ended up with a mama and papa mouse and several litters of mice—none of which I could bear to flush down the toilet or otherwise dispose of. This tale of woe is just beginning! The mother mouse was obviously a "liberated female." She quickly learned how to escape from the cage and would leave it for short periods of time. At first this was no threat because she always returned home to papa and babies. But one day she decided to liberate the entire household. It took Bruce and me several days to catch the whole litter. We're still not sure that we got all of them. We had to work fast because we feared that the brothers and sisters would begin to mate.

During the days when the mice were running free, I lived in continual fear of having one make a "guest appearance" at the wrong time. My fears became reality more than once! I can remember several times when friends fearfully stood on the kitchen counter waiting for me to corner a mouse that had chosen the wrong time to show up!

And then there was the cat the kids talked Bruce and me into getting. (Unfortunately, we didn't have it when the mice escaped!) Supposedly we had gotten one that wouldn't claw furniture and drapes. This claim proved to be true; however, this cat loved to chew things. After the ruination of many towels, shirts, socks and undies, we decided to find a new home for the cat. P.S.: Did you know that cat urine makes permanent stains on carpets? If you're in the process of filling out a research paper on cats, you'd better list that as one of its "special problems."

But before I prejudice you against cats and mice, we'd better move on!

If your child makes it past the research and the questionnaire, he needs to get ready to bring his pet home.

This involves:

Finding a space for the animal.

Preparing its home.

Getting the proper food and equipment.

And only after these things are done is he ready to carry his pet across the threshold!

Obtaining a Pet

Where is a good place to get a pet?

Go to:

Certified breeders.

Reputable pet stores.

Animal shelters.

Friends and neighbors.

or

Talk to veterinarians.

or

Answer:

Ads in the newspaper.

Announcements on local bulletin boards.

Of course some pets can be captured. Insects, amphibians, reptiles, etc., can often be found "in the wild."

With the exception of a few staff technicians in only the most progressive animal shelters, veterinarians are the only persons on the above list who have adequate education combined with experience to advise fully on environmental diet, and health care of domestic pets. My veterinarian friend says an office call fee (usually about $15) may be a good investment prior to acquiring a pet. This in-person consultation would provide the veterinarian an opportunity to assess more fully the needs and capabilities of the prospective pet owner as well as inform him of what to expect and the minimal responsibilities involved. Since the life expectancy of dogs and cats now approaches 15–20 years, adequate preparation and research could make the difference between 15–20 years of misery and 15–20 years of rewarding pet-owner relationship.

Our current pet overpopulation problem stems from widespread irresponsible pet ownership. Out of ignorance, carelessness or misguided motivation, millions of dogs and cats are allowed or caused to run loose each year and breed, populate, defecate, urinate, litter, fight and bite. Non-pet owners and responsible pet owners pay the price—they put up with and pay for animal control, litter pickup, licensing, tax-funded neutering (e.g. in the city of Los Angeles), as well as indirect costs of this public nuisance.

But no matter where your child gets his pet, he needs to make sure that it is not carrying a disease, illness or other problem that could be transferred to humans or to other pets. An examination revealing no abnormalities should be acquired from a veterinarian before the new pet is paid for in full, or, as an alternative, a statement in writing should be procured giving the new owner the option of returning the animal for full refund should it be found to be ill or defective within 72 hours after the sale. (This caution applies primarily to dogs, cats, and animals of "long" life expectancy or high cost.)

Because of the difficulty of providing proper diet and environment, but also for public health reasons, various exotic species should not be owned. (Primates contract and transmit tuberculosis, polio, measles, mumps, and other diseases to humans.) Dogs and cats transmit very few and mostly non-serious diseases to humans. Rabies is the only exception, and it is deadly; but vaccination programs are extremely effective.

Wild animals—primarily skunks, bats, and assorted carnivora —are the harboring reservoir for rabies today.

Another recommendation regarding prospective pet owners: if at all possible, have your child observe or take care of an animal similar to the one he wants before he makes his final decision. Have him volunteer to care for a pet while the owner is on vacation, or offer to take care of a friend's pet for a little while. Your child may not find anyone to cooperate with him on this, but if he does, he and his would-be pet will be better off for it.

"I'm allergic to dogs and my mom's allergic to cats, so I guess I'm just out of luck when it comes to pets," a boy complained to me.

"Nonsense!" I said. "There are other pets you can own if a dog or cat is not suitable!"

The Critter Care class formulated this list of possible pets. I'm including it in this book because all too often families limit themselves to the old stand-bys—dogs, cats, fish, and birds. Of course, some of the pets on this list are short-term pets while others are long term. Short-term pets are usually captured, kept for a short while, and then returned to nature. Long-term pets are kept until they die or are transferred to a new owner.

Possible Pets
(listed in alphabetical order)

Ants
Beetles
Birds
Canaries
Cats
Caterpillars
Chickens
Cows
Crabs

Crayfish
Crickets
Dogs
Ducks
Earthworms
Ferrets
Frogs
Geese
Gerbils (not legal to own in some states)
Goats
Goldfish
Guinea pigs
Guppies
Hamsters
Horses
Iguanas
Lizards
Mice
Mynah birds
Parakeets
Parrots
Pigeons
Rabbits
Rats
Salamanders
Sea animals
Skunks (not legal to own in some states)
Slugs
Snails
Snakes
Tadpoles
Tarantulas
Toads
Tortoises
Tropical fish
Turtles

Problems with Owning a Pet

Suppose your child has jumped through all the necessary hoops and is now the proud owner of a pet.

Slowly but surely he'll begin to understand the meaning of "continual care" and sooner or later he'll encounter a few snags.

One problem many pet owners face is what to do when a pet escapes from his cage. Most people panic whenever this happens, but panic does little to retrieve a pet. The best thing to do when a pet misplaces himself is begin a systematic search. Most pet experts recommend that the search begin in the area closest to the cage and work out from that point. This is because animals have a tendency to stay close to their source of food and water. If they should venture very far from their cage, chances are they will return sooner or later. So if the pet isn't found immediately, it is best to keep the cage door open and hope that the animal will return on its own.

In regard to animals that run away from home: again, a systematic search beginning in and around the house needs to be initiated. If it is certain that the animal has left home, a "team" of people may be needed to continue the search. Map out the neighborhood and assign each person to a specific area. Instruct the "search and rescue" team to look for the animal and talk to the people who live and work in that area. If this doesn't work, post signs and bulletins around the neighborhood alerting people to the fact that a pet has been lost. When all else fails, try putting an ad in the local newspaper or contact local radio stations that broadcast descriptions of lost and found animals.

If you suspect that your pet has been hit by a car, call the highway department because they are responsible for removing dead animals from the road.

And don't forget about the Humane Society, local pound or other animal shelters who take in lost animals. There's always a possibility that one of these organizations has your pet. But don't wait too long to call, because, generally speaking, they do not keep animals for more than three days.

Another dilemma pet owners face is what to do with pets during vacations. Several alternatives are available:

1. Hire a pet sitter to come to the house to feed, water, and care for the pet.
2. Have the pet sitter take the pet to his house and care for it there (this is recommended only for small caged animals).
3. Take the pet to a boarding kennel or a pet shelter. Because of the great chance for exposure to disease, all vaccinations should be updated at least one week prior to boarding.

In regard to these options, I tell children, "Whichever alternative you choose, make sure that your animal will receive adequate care. Talk directly to the person who will be responsible for your pet and find out whether or not he is a qualified, conscientious pet sitter. If you will be taking your pet to another place, check it out. Make sure that it is a healthy, safe place for your animal to be. If the people are reluctant to show the facilities, it is possible they may have something to hide.

Of course, there's no place like home, and more than likely your pet will not be enthusiastic about any arrangement you come up with, but, if he's in a comfortable place, chances are he'll survive until you return home.

Before you leave, make sure that you have provided the pet sitter with the necessary food and equipment your pet will need. Also, leave the name, address, and telephone number of your veterinarian with a letter giving the vet permission to care for your pet in case of an emergency.

Illness and injuries are other problems pet owners must deal with. If a pet is ill or seriously injured, it should be taken to a veterinarian so that it gets the care that it needs. Generally speaking, most pet owners are not adequately trained to diagnose and treat animals with serious physical problems.

Pets who
>   refuse to eat or drink for a long period of time
>   lack energy
>   have a dull coat, runny nose or diarrhea
>   display other abnormalities

should be referred to a vet. Also, sick or injured pets should be handled as little as possible.

Worms, fleas, ticks, and lice can be treated at home. But caution and care must be used in selecting and administering appropriate medications and supplies. Read all labels completely, including the warnings, before using. Look for species and age restrictions.

In regard to all physical problems, pet owners need to remember that, under no circumstances should a pet be left to suffer unusual amounts of discomfort and pain.

Often a child becomes disinterested in a pet or grows weary of caring for it. If your child should experience either of these two things, do everyone (including the pet) a favor and encourage your child to find a new home for his pet. Here are a few guidelines for finding a pet a new home:

DO NOT DUMP THE PET OFF SOMEWHERE in the hope that he will survive or find a new home on his own. Domesticated pets who have depended on humans for their survival will not be able to fend for themselves. Thus turning an animal "out in the cold" is a heartless, unfair thing to do. If it would survive, it might very well become a public nuisance. This problem is increasing and may well threaten our future freedom to own pets.

To find a new home for the pet, ask friends, relatives, and neighbors if they would be interested in having it. If no one responds affirmatively, advertise via local bulletin boards, newspapers or radio stations. If you are fortunate enough to find an interested party, you can either sell or give the pet away. It is important that you make sure that the pet's new home will be adequate. Carefully interview the prospective owner and if at all possible, check out the pet's future dwelling place. *DO NOT give the pet up to anyone who will neglect it in any way.*

If your efforts to find a qualified owner have been unsuccessful, try the Humane Society or other animal shelters. There is a good possibility that they will be able to help you out.

Whenever a child gets tired of caring for a pet or loses interest in it, parents should avoid the "I told you that you shouldn't have gotten that pet in the first place!" attitude. But children need to be kindly reminded of their initial commitment and they also need to be involved in finding the pet a new home. This is all a part of being a responsible pet owner.

The greatest problem most pet owners face is the final stage of the pet-owner relationship: death. This can be a real trauma for a child. Flushing a dead animal down the toilet or dumping its body in a trash can is not the best way to handle the death of a pet. Whenever a pet dies, a funeral is in order.

A lot of the feelings people go through when another person dies will be present when a pet dies. Sadness, guilt, loneliness —these feelings and more are all an integral part of coping with death. Funerals help people face and deal with these feelings. Funerals also serve as the final farewell.

So when a pet dies, be respectful. Allow your child to have a funeral, bury the body, and grieve. This, too, is part of owning a pet.

Living without Pets

If it is decided, for whatever reason, that your child cannot have a pet, he does not have to be deprived of animals altogether. He can:

Help a friend care for his pets.

Visit zoos, animal shelters and other places that have animals available to watch and touch.

Observe animals in nature.

Join the 4-H Club, Junior Humane Society, or other groups that focus on animals.

Join National Wildlife Federation and subscribe to *Ranger Rick* magazine; collect their wildlife stamps and their booklets.

There are many ways to pursue an interest in animals without actually owning one. Be creative!

Meanwhile, if by any chance you're wondering how we got rid of the skunks, we called the Humane Society to find out what we should do. They recommended that we sprinkle mothballs around and under our house! Do you know why? They said that the smell of mothballs was "offensive" to skunks. Now that's got to be one for the record!

SUMMARY

A lot of the information children receive about pets via TV, movies, books, etc., is unrealistic; thus it is important for parents to assist them in making wise decisions regarding pets. Pets make great companions, and they are entertaining and educational, but they need constant love and care.

A. A qualified pet owner is:
   1. A person who loves, respects, and understands living things.
   2. A person who is willing and able to give his pet the care that it needs.

B. Before getting a pet, a person needs to learn about it. Research can be done:
   1. At the library.
   2. At the zoo.
   3. At nature centers.
   4. At animal welfare organizations such as the Humane Society.
   5. At pet stores.

      6. By talking to a veterinarian.

      7. By talking to pet owners.

C. Before getting a pet, a person needs to know:

      1. The life span of the pet.

      2. The living conditions it requires.

      3. The diet it needs.

      4. Its habits.

      5. The care it needs.

      6. How much it will cost to purchase and maintain.

      7. Any special problems having the pet may cause.

D. Preparations need to be made before a pet is brought home. This involves:

      1. Finding a space for the animal.

      2. Preparing its home.

      3. Getting the proper food and equipment.

E. Pets can be obtained from:

      1. Certified breeders.

      2. Reputable pet stores.

      3. Animal shelters.

      4. Friends and neighbors.

      5. Veterinarians.

      6. Newspaper ads.

      7. Bulletin board announcements.

      8. Capturing them in the wild.

F. A veterinarian or an animal expert should check an animal thoroughly before the animal becomes a pet. Any sizeable investment in a pet should be contingent on this exam confirming the pet's good health and freedom from serious defects.

G. In addition to dogs, cats, fish, and birds, there are many other animals that make good pets.

H. Some of the problems pet owners face are:

      1. Losing an animal.

      2. Finding care for an animal while the owner is away on vacation.

      3. Illness, injuries and other physical problems.

    4. Finding a new home for a pet if the owner becomes disinterested or weary of caring for it.

    5. Death.

 I. A child who cannot have a pet can:

    1. Help a friend care for his pets.

    2. Visit zoos, animal shelters, etc.

    3. Observe animals in nature.

    4. Join the 4-H Club, Junior Humane Society, National Wildlife Federation, etc.

BOOKS FOR CHAPTER EIGHT

Several good books have been written on the subject of pets. Some of my favorites are:

Great Pets! An Extraordinary Guide to Usual and Unusual Family Pets, Sara Stein. New York: Workman Publishing Co., 1976.

The Kid's Pets Book, Patricia Barratt and Rosemary Dalton. Concord, Calif.: Nitty Gritty Productions, 1976.

Nature's Pets, the Care of Nature's Backyard Creatures, John Kipping. San Francisco: Troubador Press, 1975.

Your First Pet and How to Take Care of It, Carla Stevens. New York: Macmillan Publishing Co., Inc., 1974.

DANGEROUS THINGS,
         PLACES, AND
         SITUATIONS;
         FEARS;
         BAD HABITS;
         AND DESTRUCTION

9. No-No's

Several years ago, I found myself writing a new parents manual for a preschool I was directing. Automatically I included the rule, "Children are not to bring gum, candy, guns, knives or mouth toys to school." I had never given much thought to this rule before; it had been around for so long. But this time something about this rule struck me funny. "What a combination!" I thought to myself. "Everything from bubble gum to lethal weapons in one sentence!"

But that's how it is with the "no-no's" that surround our children. Out of those hundreds of prohibited objects, how is a child ever to know which are dangerous and which are not? And exactly when is he supposed to make a no-no a yes-yes? After all, he is bound to chew bubble gum sometime during his lifetime!

Dangerous Things

Christopher and Lisa have attended "open schools" since the very beginning. Generally speaking, open schools are

known for their wide range of activities. One day while visiting Christopher's classroom, I almost fainted when I saw a
four-year-old boy using a butcher knife, almost half his size,
to cut up fruit for a fruit salad. A student teacher was casually
standing by, supervising the cooking experience. "Well!" I
huffed to myself. "It's obvious that student teacher doesn't
know any better than to let a four-year-old use a butcher
knife!" Frantically, I found the head teacher and alerted her
to what was happening at the cooking table.

"Does something about that situation bother you?" the
teacher asked. For a few moments I was stunned. Finally I
managed to eke out a few words: "That little boy could cut
his finger off with that knife!" As if to say "calm down," the
teacher placed her hand on my shoulder. "Our children have
been using knives at this school for twenty years and we've
yet to have one lose a finger!" At that moment a fight erupted
in one corner of the playground, drawing the teacher abruptly
away from our conversation. Still in shock, I was pulled back
to reality by the sound of a power tool buzzing loudly in the
background. I spun around just in time to see another young
child using a power sander at the carpentry table.

That did it! If other parents were going to send their children to that school to lose their fingers and toes, that was their
business! As for me, I would be finding another school for
my children as soon as possible!

Immediately I made my way to the director's office to tell
her of my decision. The director, a wise, very sensitive lady,
saw that I was on the verge of reporting the school to the
State Board. She offered me a cup of tea and asked me to sit
down.

Angrily, I gave her a "blow-by-blow" description of what
I had witnessed in the classroom that morning. "Mrs. Wilt,"
she explained, "knives and power tools are only dangerous to
those who do not respect and know how to use them properly."
For the next half hour she carefully explained what she meant.

It took me a little while, but the whole thing started to
make sense. Competent people who respect and know how

to use "dangerous" things are seldom injured by them. Ignorance, incompetence, and disrespect are three of the major causes of accidents and injuries.

If this is true, we do not do a child a favor by removing "dangerous things" and causing him to fear them. Fear does not necessarily produce understanding, competence, and respect.

Thus, as soon as he is mentally, physically, and emotionally capable of handling dangerous things, a child should be allowed to learn about them and given opportunities to use them properly.

The key here is a child's mental and physical and emotional capabilities. Don't give a toddler a butcher knife. He's not ready to understand what the function of a butcher knife is and he would not be physically capable of handling it. In addition, he has not had enough experience to comprehend what could happen if the knife was misused.

But a young child is a different story! After observing many young children, I'm convinced that most of them are capable of handling, understanding and respecting things that are labeled "dangerous." So are older children!

My experience at Christopher's school that morning forced Bruce and me into reevaluating our entire policy regarding dangerous things.

For some time, Christopher had been wanting to explore fire and would frequently ask us to show him how to strike a match. Being indoctrinated with the concept that "children should never play with matches," Bruce and I refused to accommodate his requests. Whenever Christopher would mention matches, we would scold him, launch a lecture on the dangers of fire, and then admonish him to stay away from fire until he was older. This never satisfied Christopher.

One evening Bruce and I sat down and discussed the whole issue of "dangerous things." We concluded that if Christopher and Lisa were willing to abide by specific rules, we could allow them to explore and experience certain dangerous things. The subject was discussed at a family meeting. Chris and Lisa agreed to abide by the rules and Chris was taught how to strike a match.

Here are the rules we all agreed upon.

Chris and Lisa could explore and use anything they wanted to if:

1. They were considered by Bruce and me to be mentally, physically, and emotionally capable of using the item.
2. They would learn to use the item safely and properly.
3. They would use the item only for its intended purpose.
4. They would use the item only if an adult were present.

If a family can agree upon these rules, the next step is to formulate a list of items that would be considered "dangerous." This is so a child can never say, "Oh! I didn't realize this was a dangerous thing, so I went ahead and used it without asking you!"

Here are some of the things that may appear on a list of "Dangerous Things" (listed in alphabetical order). (*Please note: if the child is not ready to handle any or all of these items, they need to be kept completely away from him. This may mean putting these things under lock and key.*)

Aerosol cans

Axes and other hand tools

Chemicals and household cleaning agents

Electrical appliances

Explosives (such as firecrackers)

Fire

Guns

Knives and other kitchen utensils

Power tools

Razors

Recreational equipment such as slingshots, darts, archery
    sets, etc.

"But exactly when do I begin letting my children explore these things?" a father once asked me. "A child's curiosity is the key to the pace at which he should be exposed to dangerous things," I answered. Let me explain.

Curiosity motivates children to explore. It is the thing

that makes a child want to learn. This curiosity is extremely vital to the whole educational process.

But curiosity that is not respected and guided by a concerned adult can be a dangerous thing. The boy who lives across the street from us is a good example of what I mean. Roger was keenly interested in fire. He was curious about what it could do. He wanted to explore fire, but his parents sternly opposed him. So Roger decided to satisfy his curiosity on his own. One day when his parents were not home, Roger sneaked out to the garage with several matches stuffed in his back pocket. Because a caring adult was not there to give him guidance, Roger started a fire and was very badly burned. In addition, the fire destroyed several valuable things. According to the firemen who came to extinguish the fire, Roger's case was typical. He had been told never to play with fire, but disregarding his parents' commands and threats, he did it anyway.

Nine times out of ten, when this kind of thing happens, a child's curiosity is to blame. Amazingly enough, curiosity is often greater than a child's fear of being hurt or punished. This was obviously true in Roger's case.

A child who wonders about something will more than likely explore it with or without an adult. I prefer that he conduct his exploration in the presence of an adult, so that he can have the benefit of adult supervision and guidance. But this will not happen if the child suspects that his curiosity will be squelched instead of satisfied.

Christopher's curiosity about fire is a good example of this. By allowing Chris to explore fire in our presence, we eliminated the need for him to sneak. Once Christopher experimented and got his questions answered, he no longer had the burning desire (no pun intended) to explore fire. This is not to say that he stopped using it altogether. On the contrary; when a fire is needed in the fireplace or barbecue grill, Chris is always there ready to start it. If Lisa hasn't beat him to the punch, he will usually start the fire, and it is *always* with our permission and in our presence.

Incidentally, dangerous things are just like anything else in life. The fixation on exploring and using them usually vanishes once the mystery is gone. If this pattern holds true with Chris and Lisa, as I'm sure that it will, eventually they'll be arguing, "It's your turn to start the fire. I did it last time!"

Dangerous Places

How does this approach apply to dangerous places? Do we dare let children explore them? Probably not as completely as we allow them to explore dangerous things. They may not always be able to explore dangerous places with their bodies, but they can explore them with their minds. Let me explain.

One dangerous place that always concerns parents is the street. Obviously, it would not be wise to say, "Go play in the street and see what happens." The consequences may be devastating. Thus, a child has to be shown the street and told what will happen if he doesn't respect and use it properly.

The same holds true for (listed in alphabetical order):

Animal enclosures

Animal trails

Caves

Driveways and parking lots

Elevated places

Enclosed areas that have a limited circulation of air

Large or deep holes in the ground

Large or swiftly moving bodies of water

Overly polluted areas

Places which house or store large machines and equipment

Unexplored, uninhabited areas

Vehicle roadways

If you have a child who has access to any or all of the above, I recommend that you:

1. Take the child to the dangerous place.
2. Encourage him to inspect the area.
3. Explain all of the dangerous possibilities.

4. Encourage him to express his fears and ask questions.
5. Respond to his fears and answer his questions.
6. Ask him to make a commitment that he will respect the area and avoid going near it unless an adult is present or unless it is somehow made safe.

Of course, children who are too young to respond to this approach need to be kept away from the dangerous area until they are physically, mentally, and emotionally ready to handle it. This is why toddlers often require playpens, fences, and other means of protection.

Bruce and I have had a great deal of success with this approach. Most recently, our efforts were affirmed when Christopher and Lisa came rushing home with an upsetting story about "the hill." The hill is a place about two blocks from our home where the street turns into a steep hill. Riding skateboards and bikes down the hill is a thrilling experience, but extremely dangerous because the bottom of the hill turns into a blind intersection. Luckily, I had taken the time to educate Chris and Lisa about the hill, and despite peer pressure, they refused to join in the bike and skateboard races that took place on it. One day when Lisa and Chris were watching the races, they witnessed a near-collision involving a car and two bikes. The car screeched to a halt and the two bikes, in an effort to avoid the car, collided. Both of the riders were skinned up pretty badly. The whole experience caused Lisa and Chris to come running home. After every gory detail had been recounted, Chris gave me a hug. "Golly, Mom," he sighed, "I'm glad you told us about the hill a long time ago!" "Yeah," Lisa agreed, "that could have been us riding those bikes!"

Dangerous Situations

Dangerous situations are obviously more difficult to deal with than dangerous things or dangerous places. This is because a child can tactilely handle (touch) a dangerous thing and he can visually experience (look at) a dangerous place. But dangerous situations are often intangible. They are the "what if's" in a child's life. "What if a stranger approaches you? What if you see a dog with rabies running loose in the neighborhood? What if there's an earthquake?"

Children are naturally fascinated with "what if's," but they are frightened by them as well. So extreme care needs to be used when educating children about dangerous situations.

Stories, movies, books, magazine and newspaper articles, and the like are often the only means by which a child can be exposed to a dangerous situation. But these things need to be shared with extreme sensitivity. It should be a parent's goal to educate a child about dangerous situations, not scare him to death! Emphasis should be placed upon the cause and recommended response rather than the effects of a dangerous situation. In other words: If you are going to teach a child what to do during an earthquake, take time to explain what causes earthquakes and what a person should do if he experiences one. Try to avoid going into the gory details of everything that could happen to a person who experiences an earthquake. This holds true for any one of the following:

1. Acts of nature (earthquakes, tornadoes, floods, etc.).
2. Man-made disasters (fire, accidents, etc.).
3. Kidnapping and other criminal offenses.
4. Sexual offenses (molestation, rape, etc.).
5. Encounters with dangerous or unfamiliar animals.

Here's an example of what I mean, again using the earthquake to illustrate my point.

The incorrect thing to tell a child would be: "Earthquakes are really scary. They can cause buildings to collapse and huge cracks to open up in the earth. Earthquakes have been known to cause the destruction of entire cities. People have been permanently injured and even killed by earthquakes. I've read stories about people who were actually swallowed up by an earthquake. They fell into the large cracks in the earth that the 'quakes had caused. If you don't want to get injured or killed during an earthquake, you'd better be careful whenever one happens."

Several things are wrong with this approach:

1. Not enough was said about the cause of earthquakes.
2. Too much was said about the effect of earthquakes.
3. The child was given inadequate instructions regarding what he should do whenever an earthquake happens.

A more appropriate thing to tell a child would be:

"Whenever the crust of the earth shakes or trembles, it is called an earthquake. Earthquakes happen when the rock beneath the surface of the earth shifts. Underground volcanic forces also cause earthquakes. Small earthquakes happen quite often, sometimes without people ever realizing that they are happening. Larger earthquakes happen only once in a while. They often cause buildings and trees to sway or rock back and forth. This swaying back and forth can cause glass to break or things to fall off of shelves. To make sure that you are not hurt by flying glass or falling objects, you should get into a protective position during an earthquake (demonstrate the recommended position). Most of the buildings in our area are built to withstand earthquakes, but some are not. The safest place to be if you are inside a building is in a closet or doorway. This is because closets have low ceilings and doorways are less likely to collapse. If you are outside when an earthquake happens, get clear of trees and power lines."

Several things are right about this approach:

1. The child was told what causes earthquakes so that he could somewhat understand and respect them.
2. The effect of earthquakes was not the focal point of the conversation. Although it was included, it was a subtle part of this dialogue.
3. The child was told and shown specifically what he should do if ever an earthquake should happen.

Dangerous situations need to be understood and respected so that they can be dealt with appropriately. Of course, fear manages to work itself into any contemplation of a dangerous situation. This is natural and to be expected, but this fear also needs to be dealt with if a person is going to live a normal, healthy life.

Fear

Several months ago, I found myself back in my psychotherapist's office. One of the things that had driven me there was what I considered to be abnormal responses to my fantasies about danger. While driving my car, I would picture myself getting involved in an accident. The fantasy would be so real that I would catch myself cringing or even screaming out loud. Everyone does this once in a while, but I was doing it continually. Was I going crazy? I needed to know.

So, little by little, my therapist and I worked on the situation. To make the long story short, this is what we concluded.

For several years, I had experienced a major trauma approximately every six months, almost like clockwork! I went through a divorce and remarriage, had two operations for cancer, experienced two tragic accidents in my backyard (one involved the death of a five-year-old boy), both of my children were hospitalized, etc., etc. (I won't bore you with the details, but the list is quite extensive!)

Anyway, this procession of trauma had completely shattered my aura of "it can't happen to me," and I was suffering as a result.

Most adults seem somehow to feel that tragedy and trauma are things that happen to everyone else *except* them. Even when a tragedy hits, they are able to rationalize it as a "once-in-a-lifetime experience" and go on living. Generally speaking, the trauma has affected them, but it has not devastated them.

To a certain extent, this is good. If every person completely understood (or continually thought about) the potential danger that surrounded him, he would probably have a nervous breakdown or curl up and die. Thus it is important to retain the aura of "it can't happen to me" if at all possible.

"But isn't that attitude infantile?" a friend once asked. Not really, I believe. Infants have a different kind of aura: "I am invincible." Their lack of experience with pain and failure makes them almost fearless. They do not know enough to be afraid. As the infant grows older and begins to explore the world around him, he has accidents, makes mistakes, and suffers because of them. He soon becomes aware of pain and failure.

About this time, his pendulum begins to swing the other way until he gets to the place where he fears almost anything and everything.

But life goes on—and children find it difficult, if not impossible, to continue in this state of being, so they begin sorting out what is dangerous and what is not. They're never able to regain the "I am invincible" aura that they had as infants, but they finally move into the "it can't happen to me" state of being. This makes it possible for them to live a life that is not dominated and controlled by fear.

But the "it can't happen to me" aura often becomes disturbed by reality. It is a fact of life that trauma can happen to anyone, any time, and people of all ages occasionally find themselves facing this reality.

When this happens, one needs to know that much of fear comes from:

1. Not knowing.
2. Feeling a lack of control.

Children who fear the dark often do so because they do not know what is in the dark. This leaves their imagination to "fill in the blanks" and the images it conjures up are often devastating.

Children also fear things that they think they cannot control. They want to feel that they can stop anything that might possibly hurt them. Things that appear to be bigger or stronger than they are frighten them.

How do we help a child conquer such fears?

We need to:

1. Educate the child.
2. Equip him with as much control over fearful things as possible.

The best example of what I mean is the child's attitude toward water. Children who understand water and know how to swim do not fear it. This is true of most things that children are afraid of. If they understand something and feel that they have a certain amount of control over it, they will not fear it.

A child does not gain this understanding and sense of control by being forced into experiencing something that he fears. Throwing a child into the water, forcing him to slide down a slide, or making him pet an animal that he fears will only reinforce his fears.

If a child is to be educated to conquer his fear, it must be done when he is ready and at a pace he can handle. More often than not, this takes time. It also requires a great deal of love and sensitivity. On the other hand, children should not be allowed to perpetuate a fear. Parents should continually strive to expose the child to new dimensions of the thing he fears so that he can begin to understand and gain control over it.

The following is a list of fears that most children experience some time during their childhood (listed in alphabetical order).

Most children experience, at one time or another, a fear of:
Animals (especially strange or wild ones)
Being alone
Being hurt or killed by someone (burglars, thieves, murderers, kidnappers, etc.)
Being lost
Bodily harm
Change
The dark
Death
Falling
Large objects

Losing a parent or loved one
Loud noises
Natural phenomena (wind, rain, thunder, etc.)
Separation from family and friends
Supernatural or imagined beings (ghosts, goblins,
    witches, monsters)
Unfamiliar people
Unfamiliar places and surroundings
Water

If, after you have done the best you can do to educate and
equip your child to handle his fears, he is still afraid, give him
time to outgrow his fears on his own. If he retains a particular
fear for a long period of time, get help. An emotional problem
may be causing the fear and the fear will probably not go away
until the emotional problem is solved.

Let me reemphasize these important principles:

If your child has a fear,

1. Respect it. Don't make fun of him or put him down for
   having it.
2. Help him acknowledge his fear.
3. As he is ready and at a pace that he is comfortable with,
   help him learn as much as he can about the thing that
   is causing his fear.
4. Help him get in control of the thing that is causing his
   fear.
5. Give him time to overcome his fear.
6. If he does not overcome his fear in a reasonable amount
   of time, get help.

Incidentally, don't try to remove all of a child's fears. In the
first place, you won't be able to. In the second place, you
wouldn't want to, because fear is the emotion that will keep
your child from doing things that could possibly harm him.
Thus a little bit of fear is a good thing.

Bad Habits

"Margaret, stop biting your nails!"

"If Bobby wets the bed one more time, I think I'll scream!"
"Stop sucking your thumb, Eric!"
"Karen, quit chewing your hair!"
Etc., etc., etc.

You can't be around parents and children for very long without hearing these frustrated demands. They are typical of almost every parent-child relationship. Almost every child has at least one bad habit that annoys his parents. My initial response to the whole bad-habit syndrome was to develop a procedure for programming bad habits out of children.

Of course, parents responded enthusiastically, but after awhile I began to question what I was doing. It's true that a parent can train a child to start or stop almost anything—but should we?

Bad habits are often symptoms of deeper problems. Eliminating a symptom without dealing with the problem can be dangerous. Because the problem will no longer have anything to draw attention to it, it often becomes buried and never gets solved. It's a known fact that a collection of these unsolved problems can cause neurotic disorders.

Thus the most important part of dealing with your child's bad habits is dealing with whatever is causing them.

Some of the common causes of bad habits are (in alphabetical order):

Anxiety
Boredom
Fatigue
Feelings of inadequacy
Feelings of inferiority
Frustration
Hunger
The inability to express oneself
Insecurity
Need for attention
Rejection
Restlessness
Unchanneled energy

Your child's bad habit could possibly be a result of one or a combination of these things. It could also be a result of something that is not on this list.

In any case, a bad habit is usually an outlet for a child, one way of relieving tension and dealing with a problem. If you can help your child to solve his problems, his bad habits will often disappear.

The key is pinpointing the cause of the bad habit so that it can be dealt with. Observe your child carefully for an extended period of time (a week or more). Whenever he engages himself in his bad habit, make note of:

1. What time of the day it is.
2. Who is with him.
3. How he is feeling.
4. Exactly what happens before, during, and after he engages in his bad habit.

A week's careful observation should give you some insight into why your child is doing what he is doing. If you can't put it all together, however, it's time to get professional help. Get together with a qualified children's psychologist, therapist, pediatrician, or educator. One or more of these specialists will probably be able to help determine what's causing the problem and what you can do to help your child solve it.

Meanwhile—back at the ranch—relax! Bugging your child about his bad habit will only intensify the problem. Remember that a child's bad habits are similar to the bad habits of adults, in that both are outlets. They are ways of relieving inner tensions and dealing with problems.

Most bad habits that occur during childhood cycle themselves out. After all, do you know very many adults who suck their thumbs or bang their heads on the floor when they are angry? Remember this the next time you ask yourself, "Is my child going to be doing this all the rest of his life?"

Destroying Valuable Things

And now for the "no-no" of all "no-no's"—Mother's crystal vase!

Every parent has one or two prized possessions that rank high on the list of what should be saved in case of fire. If these possessions are to survive childhood, I recommend that:

1. They be completely removed from a child's reach until he is able to understand and value it as a "prized possession."
2. When the child becomes "of age," the prized possession can be put on display, but only after
   a. The child has been educated as to the importance and value of the prized possession.
   b. The child has been told exactly what he can and cannot do with the prized possession.
   c. The child completely understands what will happen to him if the rules regarding the prized possession are disobeyed.

Take it from a weary warrior. After losing an antique crystal vase, an imported china figurine, and several other priceless possessions, I learned that it is better to be safe than sorry.

SUMMARY

In regard to dangerous things:

A. Dangerous things are only dangerous to those who do not respect and know how to use them properly.
B. Ignorance, incompetence, and disrespect in handling dangerous things are three of the major causes of accidents and injuries.
C. As soon as a child is mentally, physically, and emotionally capable of handling dangerous things, he should be allowed to learn about them and given opportunities to use them properly. (Please note: If the child is not ready to handle any item, keep it entirely away from him. This may mean putting it under lock and key.)
D. Children should be able to explore and use anything they want to if:

1. Their parents consider them to be mentally, physically and emotionally capable of using the item.
2. They learn to use the item safely and properly.
3. They use the item only for its intended purpose.
4. They use the item only if an adult is present.
E. A child's curiosity is the key to the pace at which he should be exposed to dangerous things.

In regard to dangerous places:
A. Children may not be able to explore dangerous places with their bodies, but they can with their minds.
B. Guidelines for exposing a child to dangerous places:
   1. Take the child to the dangerous place.
   2. Encourage him to inspect the area.
   3. Explain all of the dangerous possibilities.
   4. Encourage him to express his fears and ask questions.
   5. Respond to his fears and answer his questions.
   6. Ask him to make a commitment that he will respect the area and avoid going near it unless an adult is present or unless it is somehow made safe.

In regard to dangerous situations:
A. Dangerous situations are often intangible. They are the "what if's" in a child's life.
B. It should be a parent's goal to educate a child about dangerous situations, not scare him to death.
C. To do this, emphasis should be put on the *cause* and recommended response rather than the effects of a dangerous situation.

In regard to fear:
A. Infants have an aura of "I am invincible" based on the fact that they have had very little experience with pain and failure.
B. As a child grows older and begins to explore the world around him, his accidents and mistakes make him aware of pain and failure and cause him to be fearful.

C. A child's aura of "it can't happen to me" often becomes disturbed by reality.

D. Fear comes from:
   1. Not knowing, and
   2. Feeling a lack of control.

E. Parents should handle a child's fear by:
   1. Respecting it. Don't make fun of the child or put him down for having it.
   2. Helping him acknowledge his fear.
   3. As he is ready and at a pace that he is comfortable with, educate him as much as you can about the thing that is causing his fear.
   4. Helping him get in control of the thing that is causing his fear.
   5. Giving him time to overcome his fear.
   6. If he does not overcome his fear in a reasonable amount of time, get help.

In regard to bad habits:

A. Bad habits are often symptoms of deeper problems.

B. The most important part of dealing with your child's bad habits is dealing with whatever is causing them.

C. Bad habits are an "outlet" for a child to relieve tension and deal with problems.

D. To pinpoint the cause of a bad habit, observe your child for an extended period of time. Make note of:
   1. What time of day it is.
   2. Who is with him.
   3. How he is feeling.
   4. Exactly what happens before, during and after he engages himself in his bad habit.

E. Get professional help if you cannot get to the root of your child's problem on your own.

F. Do not bug your child about his bad habit. This will only intensify the problem.

G. Bad habits that occur during childhood usually cycle themselves out.

In regard to destroying valuable things:

A. Remove prized possessions from a child's reach until he is able to understand and value them.

B. When the child is old enough, give him careful instructions about the prized possession so that he will not damage or destroy it.

10. The Boob-Tube Blues

Carlo and Robert were two teen-age boys from the same family. They were great guys and both of them related extremely well to Chris and Lisa, so we asked them if they would take turns babysitting for us. At first Chris and Lisa were thrilled to have Carlo and Robert take care of them, but as time went on, their enthusiasm waned.

One evening we announced to the children that Robert would be caring for them while we went out to dinner.

"Oh, no!" moaned Christopher. Shocked by his response, I said, "But I thought you *liked* Carlo and Robert!"

"I do!" Chris responded. "But whenever they babysit us, all they want to do is watch TV!" At this point Lisa chimed in. "Yeah!" she said. "They even like the commercials!"

The more we got to know the boys, the more we began to understand *why* this was true. Carlo and Robert's parents had decided that because TV was such an "abomination," there would be no television set in their home. As a result of this decision, Carlo and Robert became "fixated" on TV and whenever they had access to one they could never get enough.

This is the problem with "throwing the baby out with the bath water." It is true that television can have a negative effect on children, but only if it is not used properly. As with everything in life, television can have a positive or negative influence, depending upon how it's used.

Facts about TV Viewing

You've probably heard this before, but for the sake of refreshing your memory, let's take it once again—from the top! Statistics show that:
- —By the time the average American child has finished high school, he will have spent 15,000 hours watching TV. (This is more time than he will have spent doing anything else—except sleeping!)
- —During the 15,000 hours the child will have been exposed to approximately 350,000 commercials and he will have watched approximately 18,000 murders.

Is it any wonder TV is so influential in the life of a child?

Effects of TV Watching

What does all of this TV do to a child? Many pediatricians, therapists, and educators maintain that too much TV or TV that is watched without parental guidance can:
- —Influence children to want and possibly buy things that are not good for them.
- —Become an escape from reality.
- —Become a substitute for companionship and active play and thus inhibit creativity and personal growth.
- —Cause children to become aggressive and in some cases violent.
- —Influence children into doing things that are not good for them or for other people.
- —Cause a child to have an unrealistic view of the world.

Needless to say, these effects eventually take their toll on the individual child as well as the society as a whole. But before you decide to get rid of your TV, let us examine the other side of the coin—the positive side.

Most pediatricians, therapists, and educators also maintain that television, when used properly, can:

—Bring a family together.
—Stimulate conversation between family members.
—Allow a child to relax and "unwind."
—Expose children to new concepts and ideas.
—Expand a child's perception of the world.
—Reinforce educational facts and concepts.

So how does one make sure that TV's effect on one's life is positive rather than negative? The key is to:

—Watch only those things that have quality and integrity.
—Use moderation in watching TV.

Selecting TV Programs Wisely

The National Association for Better Broadcasting has established the following standards for evaluating television programs as shown in the chart on pages 138–39.

In addition to these standards, there is another criterion for selecting appropriate programs. If the program involves a movie, you can tell whether or not it will be something your child should watch by how the movie has been rated by the motion picture industry.

G-rated movies are ones children can understand. In addition, any sex activity is shown in the context of a loving relationship. Violence is presented as a force of law and order (not as a way of solving problems) and there is always a clear distinction between right and wrong.

PG-rated movies are ones in which children can understand the main theme without understanding underlying themes. Sex is sometimes referred to outside the context of a loving rela-

STANDARD	DESIRABLE—IF:	UNDESIRABLE—IF:
1. Does it appeal to the audience for whom intended?	It gives information and/or entertainment related to real life situations or interests.	Dull, boring, not related to experience or interests; exaggerated beyond believability.
2. Does it meet people's needs for entertainment and action?	Wholesome adventure, humor, fantasy, suspense.	Unnecessary morbid emphasis on cruelty and violence; loud, crude, or vulgar.
3. Does it add to one's understanding and appreciation of himself, others, the world?	Sincere; constructive; informative; balanced picture of life; encourages decent human relations; fair to races, nations, religions, labor and management.	One-sided propaganda; arouses prejudice; plays on emotions and lack of knowledge.
4. Does it encourage worthwhile ideals, values, and beliefs? (family life, etc.)	Upholds acceptable standards of behavior; promotes democratic and spiritual values, respect for law, decency, service.	Glamorizes crime, indecency, intolerance, greed, cruelty; encourages bad material success, personal taste, false standards of vanity, intemperance, immorality.
5. Does the program stimulate constructive activities?	Promotes interests, skills, hobbies; encourages desire to learn more, to do something constructive, to be creative, to solve problems, to work and to live with others.	Gives details of theft, robbery, smuggling and other crime; if problems are solved by brute force, or if situations are resolved by chance rather than by logical story development.

STANDARD	DESIRABLE—IF:	UNDESIRABLE—IF:
6. Does it have artistic qualities?	Skillful production as to music, script, acting, direction, art work, sets, sound effects, photography.	Poorly done job; confusing; hard to follow; action too fast, too slow; sound too loud, too low.
7. Is the commercial acceptable?	Presented with courtesy and good taste, reasonably brief, in harmony with content and sound volume of program; delivered by announcer.	Too loud, too many, deceptive; poor taste in content and treatment.

ADDITIONAL STANDARDS APPLIED SPECIFICALLY
TO CHILDREN'S PROGRAMS

1. Crime is never suitable as a major theme of a program for children.
2. There should be immediate resolution of suspense, and the program should avoid undue stress or fear.
3. A clear differentiation should be made between fantasy and fact.

tionship, but this does not involve the main characters. Violence and right and wrong must be treated in the same way as in a G-rated film.

R-rated movies are adult movies that children may not understand. These movies tell stories of people and their individual lives, and are not to suggest in any way that other people imitate them. The rules that apply to G and PG ratings in regard to sex, violence, and right and wrong do not apply to R-rated movies.

X-rated movies are adult movies that handle sex, violence, crimes, or profanity in ways that do not meet any of the standards mentioned above.

As applied to admission practices at local theaters, these ratings mean:

G—All ages admitted

PG—All ages admitted, but parental guidance is recommended

R—Persons under 17 years of age must be accompanied by an adult in order to be admitted

X—No person under 17 years of age will be admitted

With the standards set up by the NABB and the movie industry ratings in mind, I recommend that parents sit down with their child *before* turning the TV on and decide which programs are all right for him to watch. I know of some families who take the time to do this every evening. Others do it once a week when the TV program guide is published.

However it is handled, careful selections need to be made and children should not be left to decide for themselves on suitable viewing.

Deciding How Much Time Will Be Spent Watching TV

Some studies suggest that children should not watch TV for more than one hour per day, while other studies sanction anything up to four hours per day as okay. As far as I'm concerned, I think that an amount of time in between these two numbers is acceptable. But in making the final decision, parents and children need to know and respect the fact that it is not mentally or physically good for any child to watch TV for more than two hours at a time. In addition, it should be remembered that when children are passively involved in watching TV, they are not actively involved in other things. Life is far more productive for those who live it rather than observe it.

Making TV Safe

In regard to your child's physical safety while watching TV:
1. Have your child sit a safe distance from the television set. To determine what is "safe," measure the width of

the TV screen and multiply that number by five for the minimum distance, in inches.

2. Do not allow your child to wear sunglasses while watching TV.
3. Do not allow your child to watch TV in a completely dark room.
4. Do not put the television set in a place where there will be glare or reflections from lights or windows.
5. Make sure that the volume is not turned above a normal level.

In regard to your child's mental safety while watching TV: The mental anguish children can suffer from watching TV is largely the result of:

1. TV commercials.
2. Violence on TV.
3. The unrealistic way in which TV portrays life.

To help your child survive these things, try to watch TV with him (or be somewhere close by) so that you can put these things into perspective for him. Ultimately it will be up to you to point out the fallacies and inconsistencies in TV commercials. It will be up to you to explain the violence he sees, and it will be up to you to bring him down from the clouds and back into reality.

Ask him questions!

"Do you think that what that man is saying is true? Why?"

"What would happen if a person did that in real life?"

"Do things like that really happen?"

Make him think! Turn him into a critical observer. Help him become an intelligent viewer. Any amount of time you spend doing this will be well worth it in the end.

The old "monkey see–monkey do" adage really applies to children and TV. Parents who are TV-aholics cannot expect their children to abstain from watching TV or even control their TV habits. If you want your child to develop a healthy attitude toward TV, develop your own maturity toward TV and then model that attitude to your child.

SUMMARY

A. Television can have a positive or negative influence on a child's life, depending upon how it is used.

B. The enormous amount of time children spend watching TV will inevitably have an impact on them.

C. Too much TV or TV watched without parental guidance can be detrimental to children.

D. Television when used properly can enhance a child's life.

E. The standards set up by the National Association for Better Broadcasting and the movie ratings can help parents and children decide which programs would be appropriate to watch.

F. Most children can handle one to four hours of TV per day, but they should not watch TV for more than two hours at one time.

G. In order to make TV a physically safe experience for your child:

   1. Make sure he sits far enough away from the television set.
   2. Do not let him wear sunglasses while watching TV.
   3. Do not let him watch TV in a dark room.
   4. Do not put the television set where it will receive glare or reflections from the windows or lights.
   5. Do not allow your child to turn the volume up above a normal level.

H. In order to make TV mentally safe, watch TV with your child and put the following into perspective for him:

   1. TV commercials.
   2. Violence on TV.
   3. The unrealistic way in which TV portrays life.

I. If you want your child to have a healthy attitude toward TV, you must model that attitude.

BOOKS FOR CHAPTER TEN

For parents who are interested in doing some more research on children and TV, I highly recommend these two books:

The Early Window, Effects of Television on Children and Youth, Robert M. Liebert, John M. Neale and Emily S. Davidson. New York: Pergamon Press, Inc., 1973.

The Family Guide to Children's Television, Evelyn Kaye. New York: Random House, 1974.

A good book for your child to read on this subject is *I Am Not a Short Adult! Getting Good at Being a Kid* by Marilyn Burns (Boston: Little, Brown and Co., 1977).

11. Cake, Ice Cream, and Chaos

Anita Lobel has written several wonderful children's books. My favorite is the one entitled *A Birthday for the Princess*. It's a story about a "grand birthday party" that was given in honor of a princess's birthday. Carefully planned by the king and queen, the party included such things as:

The Sterling String Ensemble

The Kapusta Octet

The Noctambule Nonsense Dancers

The Juvenile Juggling Team of Pergolesi, Pergolesi and Smith

The Philistine Palaver Poetry Players

The Fantastic Rope Trick Fakir from Fandango

Important guests attended the event and everyone was duly impressed—everyone, that is, except the princess. Bored by the program and feeling badly that her friends (a lowly organ grinder and a monkey) were not allowed to come to her party, she complained to her mother: "But I thought this was *my* party." The queen couldn't be bothered. She silenced the princess and ignored her complaints.

The resourceful princess persisted and finally found a way to sneak her friends into the grand ballroom.

> When the princess was discovered dancing with a monkey and not sitting straight in her chair, a great uproar began.
> The party turned into a disaster, and the organ grinder and the monkey were thrown into the dungeon. "Ungrateful child!" the queen screamed at the princess. "What a way to behave at such a nice party."
> With bruised ankles and broken instruments, the performers left the palace. The grandmothers and uncles and aunts and cousins went to bed because the party was over. The princess lay in bed and cried and cried.

The story goes on, but in fairness to Ms. Lobel, I'll leave you to read the intriguing ending in her book.

A Birthday for the Princess is a fantasy, but its message is painfully true.

All too often, in an effort to impress their friends and relatives, parents plan "grand birthday parties" without giving much thought to the needs and desires of the child. Indeed, these events impress the adults, but they often lose the children. Inevitably, the guest of honor ends up saying, "But I thought this was *my* party!"—to which the parents respond, "Ungrateful child!"

Needless to say, such encounters do not lend themselves to pleasant childhood memories.

What is a parent to do?

The Criteria for a Good Party

I had to face this question when Christopher turned six. At this stage of the game, he had become a well-seasoned party-goer, and he, along with the rest of his peers, had become extremely opinionated on the subject of birthday parties.

Realizing that just any old thing would never do, I decided that I had better consult Christopher before I planned his sixth birthday party.

"What do you like about birthday parties?" I asked him.

"First, let's talk about what I don't like!" he suggested.

"Okay," I responded, and this is what he said:

"I don't like hats. They're embarrassing to wear.

"I don't like decorations. No one cares about them.

"I don't like prizes that break.

"I don't like the parties where I have to dress up, and I don't like games that are dumb."

"Well, what *do* you like?" I questioned.

"I like fun games, good food, and neat prizes," he said.

Christopher's clearly defined answers to my questions intrigued me. "Is he an exceptional child in this area?" I wondered. "Or is he typical?"

I began to talk to other children regarding the subject of parties. I was amazed to find that most of them were as opinionated about parties as Chris. In addition, their answers were surprisingly similar to Christopher's answers. Of course, responses varied from child to child, but one thing was for sure: children three years of age and up who have attended parties *know* what they like and don't like.

The Basic Components of a Party

My casual research project turned out to be very interesting, and the information I gathered affected the way I have since handled Christopher's and Lisa's parties.

I've learned a lot since Chris's sixth birthday party.

Party Invitations

Hand-made party invitations make a hit with mothers, but children are often unimpressed. The commercial invitations featuring popular characters and animals are more readily accepted. Most of these invitations are relatively inexpensive, but if you're pinching pennies and would rather not buy invitations, either you or your child can invite the guests in person, by telephone or with a written note. If you write your own invitation, be sure to include:

1. Who the party is for.
2. What the party is for.
3. When the party will start.
4. When the party will be over.
5. Where the party will be held (give address and phone number).

You may also want to indicate what type of clothing will be appropriate.

Of course, it's always fun to get things in the mail, but mailing invitations can get awfully expensive, and children seem to respond just as well to invitations that have been personally delivered. Thus, if money is an issue, I wouldn't recommend spending any on stamps. However, let me caution you: The main disadvantage of personally delivered invitations is that they often fail to make it home. To compensate for this, you may want to place follow-up phone calls to the mothers of the children who have been invited to the party.

Party Decorations

When I asked the children to assign priorities to the various facets of a party, the decorations ended up at the bottom of the list. Balloons hanging from the ceiling were "good for popping" and crepe paper streamers were "fun to stretch," but according to children, that is about all they are good for.

One mother disagreed. "But decorations set the mood for the party!" she insisted. Perhaps this mother is right, but if you've only got so much time and money to spend on a party, most children would vote against your spending it on decorations.

Party Games and Activities

The enthusiastic "Mom! You'll never guess what we did at

the party!" is usually a result of exciting party games and activities. Don't skimp on these things when you're planning and preparing a party, because the time and money you invest in the games and activities will really pay off.

I was extremely interested in finding out exactly what children liked to do at parties. By talking to several of them, I discovered that children enjoy:

>Being entertained.
>
>Going places.
>
>Doing special things.

The kind of entertainment children like is:

>Movies (these can either be rented or borrowed from a local library).
>
>Magic shows.
>
>Puppet shows.
>
>Clown performances.

(Magic, puppet and clown shows can be done by nonprofessionals in the community. In most cases, it can be some older child or teenager who will perform for a nominal fee.)

Children like parties where they go:

>To amusement parks
>
>Bike riding
>
>Bowling
>
>To the circus
>
>Hiking and exploring
>
>Horseback riding
>
>Miniature golfing
>
>To the movies
>
>To parks
>
>To restaurants specializing in foods children enjoy (i.e. ice cream and pizza parlors, etc.)
>
>Skating
>
>Swimming
>
>To the zoo

At the top of the list of favorite party games and activities you'll usually find:

Candy or penny hunts (something like Easter egg hunts, only done with pennies instead of eggs)
Piñatas
Scavenger hunts
Treasure hunts
Unique forms of individual and team competition

Children do not like doing everyday things at parties. The games and activities they play at home and at school are fun—but not suitable for parties.

Recently I've come across some clever ideas for children's parties. They're somewhat different from the old stand-bys and you may want to consider using one the next time your child wants to have a party.

1. *The Toy Party.* Several good books have been written showing children how to make toys out of free or inexpensive materials. Provide the necessary materials and help the children make several toys. Then encourage them to play with their creations. You may even want to set up a few contests and have the children use their toys.

2. *The Puppet Party.* Several good books have been written about puppets children can make and use. Again, provide the materials and help the children make their own puppets. Then encourage them to put on puppet shows for each other. To add to the fun, take snapshots or moving pictures of the puppets and the presentations.

3. *The Cooking Party.* There are hundreds of children's cookbooks on the market. Either purchase one or borrow one from the library. Then provide the ingredients for several of the recipes. Let the children cook their own food and eat it.

4. *The Water Party.* This is especially great for summer parties. Tell the children to wear bathing suits to the party. Have water balloons and squirt-gun fights; provide safe water toys and play games in the sprinklers. The children will love it.

5. *The Kite Party.* Get hold of one of the many books written on kite-making. Provide the necessary materials; then help each child make his own kite. When the kites are finished,

let the children fly them. (P.S. If the children aren't adept enough to make their own kites, you may want to buy each one of them an inexpensive kite and let them fly it.)

6. *The Paper Airplane Party.* You'll need plenty of paper for this one! Get a paper-airplane book with the instructions for making paper airplanes. Have each child make several paper airplanes, then involve them in paper airplane contests (which airplane can go the highest, the longest, make the most loops, etc.).

7. *The Movie Party.* Get hold of a home movie camera. Have the children write a simple script and then make a simple movie. Invite the children back in a couple of weeks for the movie premiere.

8. *The New Games Party.* There's a book entitled *New Games* edited by Andrew Fluegelman. The unique games proposed in this book reinforce the concept "Play Hard, Play Fair, Nobody Hurt." The activities in this book are indeed new and the children at your party will *love* playing them.

9. *The Arts and Crafts Party.* Select several unique art or craft projects. Provide the necessary materials and supplies; then encourage the children to do the projects.

10. *The Bike Skills Party.* Have the guests bring their bikes to the party. Set up an obstacle course for them to ride through; have them take a short bike hike, or do a scavenger hunt on bikes. Set up bike contests and award ribbons to the winner. (If the children aren't yet riding bikes, have them use skates, skateboards, wagons, trikes, etc.)

Prizes and Party Favors

According to one child I talked to, "Party favors make a party last a little longer." How true this is! Substantial party prizes and favors will last and provide many hours of fun for the party guests long after the party is over.

Flimsy prizes and party favors that can't be used or that break easily are frustrating for children, and things that are dangerous, messy, or make loud noises are frustrating for parents. Thus, party prizes and favors need to be selected with care.

Here is a list of party prizes and favors that are sure to please both children and parents; some can be made, others purchased:

Bag of balloons
Bag of marbles
Ball and cup
Ball and jacks
Ball and paddle
Balsa wood airplane
Bubbles
Button spinner
Candy
Card games
Coin purse
Coloring book and crayons
Gyroscope
Harmonica
Inexpensive jewelry
Jump rope
Kaleidoscope
Kazoo
Kite
Lip gloss
Magic rocks
Magic slate
Magnet
Magnifying glass
Nerf ball
Octascope
Paint-with-water book and brush
Paper dolls
Pen or pencil set
Pinwheel

Pocket doll
Punch ball
Puppets (hand, finger, rod, or novelty)
Puzzles
Rubber ball
Rub-on transfers
Silly string
Slinky
Small can of play dough
Small transportation toys
Special toothbrushes
Squirt guns
Stickers
Sticker books
Styrofoam gliders
Tablets of paper
Tattoos
Toiletries (perfume, soap, bubble bath)
Toys
Wiffle ball
Yo-yo

You may want to give one or a combination of these things, wrapped or tied up in a small paper bag. Hats, buttons, and things of this nature are not always readily accepted; some children find these things embarrassing to wear.

One problem with all party favors and prizes is that they often get misplaced or end up in the wrong person's possession before the party is over. For this reason I recommend passing out the goodies just before the children go home.

Another clever idea that will help you keep the favors and prizes straight is what I call the "party bag." It is nothing more than a large grocery bag that can either be decorated or left plain. In any case, there is one bag for every guest. Each child's name is written on his own bag. When a guest arrives, he is shown his bag. If he is wearing a coat or sweater or if he has brought along a purse or small toy, he places it in his bag. When the parents come, they are given their child along with his bag.

Party bags can make "pick-up time" a lot smoother. They also prevent children from leaving their things behind.

Party Refreshments

"Refreshments are not all that expensive," one mother observed. "It's the paper plates, napkins, and cups that get out of hand!"

"Then don't get the paper plates, napkins and cups!" I responded. "Paper goods can add up fast, and, like party decorations, they are seldom appreciated by the children."

The mother continued, "If I don't get plates, napkins, and cups, what will I serve the food on?"

"Nothing!" I answered. "Try to serve refreshments that do not require plates, cups, and napkins."

There are several foods that meet this qualification:

Brownies

Candy apples

Canned pudding

Chinese finger gels

Cookies

Cupcakes

Doughnuts

Frozen yogurt (cups, bars, push-ups, etc.)

Fruit leather

Ice cream novelties (sandwiches, cups, bars, etc.)

Ice cream or yogurt cones

Individual bags of nuts, pretzels, chips, caramel popcorn, etc.

Individual cans of fruit juice

Individual cans of fruit punch

Individual cans of pop

Popcorn balls

Popsicles

Rice Krispie treats

Sweet rolls

S'mores

In addition to being easy to serve, most of these foods require a minimum of preparation and clean-up.

If, after being exposed to the alternatives, your child insists on having cake and ice cream, get the most inexpensive paper goods money can buy, because unlike adults, children do not pay attention to what the food is being served on. They are much more interested in the food itself.

In regard to the "birthday cake," some kids really enjoy beautifully decorated cakes. However, most children couldn't care less. Again, children are not nearly so concerned about what a cake looks like as they are about how it tastes.

Another alternative to serving the traditional cake and ice cream is serving refreshments that the children prepare themselves. Children enjoy working with food almost as much as they enjoy eating it. Thus, you may want to let the party guests:

1. Frost and decorate their own cupcakes, cookies, or doughnuts.
2. Put together their own ice cream sundae or banana split.
3. Mix their own juice concoction out of a variety of fruit juices.
4. Pull taffy.
5. Assemble fruit kabobs.
6. Churn homemade ice cream.

You can cut corners by eliminating the paper goods and getting undecorated cakes, but whatever you do, spend most of your party budget on the food. Why? Because according to most children, refreshments are one of the most important things at a party.

Incidentally, before I leave the subject of party refreshments, I want to say that I consider "junk foods" okay for parties. As you will find in the thirteenth chapter of this book, I recommend giving children nutritious food most of the time.

However, parties are special occasions and are perfect opportunities to deviate from the norm.

If you're planning to provide breakfast, lunch, or dinner for your guests, refer to the suggested food lists in chapter 13 for ideas about what you can serve.

Other Important Things to Consider When Planning a Party

Time Lengths

A party for children should not last *less* than two hours or *more* than three hours. (Of course, excursions and slumber parties are exceptions to this rule.) Children feel cheated if a party is less than two hours, but they tend to get wild and out of control at parties that go past three hours. Two, two-and-a-half and three-hour parties work out best.

There are advantages and disadvantages to both mornings and afternoons for party times. Morning parties are good for children who usually nap in the afternoon, but it's a let-down to have the party over so early in the day. Afternoon parties give children something to look forward to, but children tend to be a little more tired and grumpy during this time of the day.

Morning parties are usually held some time between 9:30 and 11:30. Anything earlier than 9:30 usually means that the party will include breakfast. Afternoon parties happen sometime between 1:00 and 5:00. Parties that go later than 5:00 usually mean that dinner will be served to the guests. Generally speaking, lunch is expected if the party goes on during the lunch hour (12:00 to 1:00).

It's good to keep these things in mind when you decide when and how long your party will be.

Number of Guests

Children tend to invite too many friends to their birthday

party, perhaps because of the number of presents they hope to receive. Other reasons cause them to overload the guest list for other parties. Thus, parents need to step in when the guest list is being formulated.

Generally speaking, there needs to be at least one adult for every:

4 infants and toddlers

6 two- to six-year-olds

8 to 10 seven- to twelve-year-olds.

Additional children require additional adults. Thus the number of children your child invites to his party is quite dependent upon how many adults you can round up to help you. I've known parents who trade their services. One parent will help a friend supervise a party in exchange for the friend helping him. In most cases this works out well.

Other factors that influence the length of a guest list are:

The amount of money that can be spent on the party.

The amount of space available for the party. (Allow approximately 35 square feet per child.)

Unfortunately, some children evaluate the success of a party on the basis of how many people attend it. Parents should not be intimidated by this. "Quality is better than quantity" when evaluating a party.

Choosing a Place for a Party

Remember that, at their best, and even when trying hard not to, children can spill things, drop things, bump into things and trip over things.

A wise parent will keep this in mind when deciding where to have his child's party. Carpeted rooms with lovely furniture and precious possessions are unsuitable.

The best place to have a children's party is outdoors where they can run and play freely. In situations where there is not enough outdoor space or where the weather is bad, the party will need to be moved inside. But indoor parties need to be held in rooms that can take a certain amount of abuse. If such a room is not available at home, the party should take place away from home.

Parents of the guests need to be informed as to where their child will be during the party. If the party is to be held away from home, the exact location should be included in the invitation or the parents should be informed when they drop their children off at the party.

Clothes to Wear to a Party

It's true that some boys and girls enjoy dressing up, but these children are usually the exception rather than the rule. So unless the party is specifically a "dress-up affair," do everyone a favor and specify that the guests wear "casual" or "play" clothes.

Other Facets of a Party

Name tags: No one—even a child—likes to be called "Hey, you!" To avoid this, provide name tags for the children to wear. You can buy self-adhesive name tags at stationery stores, but these may be small and consequently difficult to see from a distance. I find that masking tape works out extremely well. I buy the tape that is approximately 2 inches wide and then write the child's name on it in letters approximately 1½ inches tall. By the time the party is over, I've almost memorized every child's name and, needless to say, it really makes a hit.

Helping hands: No matter how large or small your party is, you're going to need help. Another adult would be great, but an older child or teen-ager will work out fine. Just make sure that whoever you get is a good sport and enjoys working with children. A grouch will never do!

Receiving presents: Ask almost any child what he liked most about his birthday party and he'll say, "The presents."

Because presents are so important to children, help preserve them by putting them away in a safe place immediately after they have been opened. If you leave them out for everyone at the party to play with, many of the gifts will get lost or broken. Picking up the broken pieces of a new toy is a sad way to end a party—don't let it happen. Your child will be glad that you intervened.

Giving presents: The present your child takes to a birthday party should be one that he is proud to give. Nothing is more embarrassing than giving a present that is inferior to the ones brought by the other children. To avoid this embarrassment, talk to your child before you buy a gift and let him help you select it.

Planning Parties That Children Will Enjoy

Whatever you do, consult your child first! From the very beginning, bring him in on the planning of his party so it will be one that he enjoys and is proud of. Remember, a well-planned party can contribute greatly to his feeling important and cared for.

In closing . . .

> Happy Birthday to you,
> You belong in a zoo!
> You look like a monkey,
> You act like one, too!

Now these words may not seem funny to you, but when they are sung to the tune of "Happy Birthday to You," children crack up with laughter! That's the way it is with a lot of things. Children enjoy things that adults could never possibly enjoy and vice-versa. Remember this the next time you plan a party for children!

SUMMARY

A. All too often, parents, in an effort to impress their friends and relatives, plan "grand birthday parties" without giving much thought to the needs and desires of the child. Indeed, these events impress the adults, but they often end up losing the children.

B. According to children, the criteria for a good party are:
1. Fun games and activities.
2. Good food.
3. Quality favors and prizes.

In regard to party invitations:

A. Children can be invited to a party:
1. In person.
2. By telephone.
3. By written invitation.

B. Whether written invitations are hand-made or commercial, personally delivered or mailed, make sure they include:
1. Who.
2. What.
3. When.
4. Where (include the address of where the party will be located).
5. Your telephone number.
6. Recommended dress.

In regard to party decorations:

A. If you've only got so much time and money to spend on a party, most children would vote against your spending it on decorations.

In regard to party games and activities:

A. Don't skimp on these things when you're planning and preparing a party because they are one of the most important parts of a party.

B. When it comes to parties, children like to:
   1. Be entertained.
   2. Go places.
   3. Do special things.
C. Children do not like doing "every day" things at parties. The games and activities they play at home and school are fun, but not suitable for parties.
D. Here is a list of parties that are somewhat different from the old standbys:
   1. The toy party.
   2. The puppet party.
   3. The cooking party.
   4. The water party.
   5. The kite party.
   6. The paper airplane party.
   7. The movie party.
   8. The New Games party.
   9. The arts-and-crafts party.
   10. The bike skills party.

In regard to prizes and favors:
A. Substantial prizes and party favors will last and provide many hours of fun for the party guests long after the party is over.
B. Avoid getting:
   1. Flimsy things that can't be used or break easily.
   2. Things that are dangerous, messy or make loud noises.
C. Hats, buttons and things of this nature are often embarrassing for children to wear.

In regard to refreshments:
A. Refreshments are an important part of a party. When deciding what to serve, try to select foods that:
   1. Require a minimum of preparation.
   2. Do not require paper plates, napkins, and cups.
   3. Are easy to serve.
   4. Are easy to clean up after.

B. Children are not very concerned with what a cake looks like. They are more concerned with how it tastes.
C. Another alternative to serving the traditional cake and ice cream is serving refreshments that the children prepare themselves.

In regard to the time allotted for a party:
A. A children's party should not be less than two hours or more than three hours.
B. Good party times are:
  1. Morning: sometime between 9:30 and 11:30.
  2. Afternoon: sometime between 1:00 and 5:00.
C. Having parties at other times during the day usually means that a meal is included.

In regard to the number of guests to invite to a party:
A. Guest lists are dependent upon:
  1. The number of adults available to help supervise the party.
  2. The amount of space that is available for the party.

In regard to choosing a place for a party:
A. The best place for a children's party is outdoors.
B. Indoor parties should take place in rooms that can take a certain amount of abuse.
C. If such a room or outdoor space is not available at home, the party should take place away from home.

In regard to the clothes children wear to a party:
A. In most cases, children prefer and should be allowed to wear "casual" or "play" clothes to parties.

In regard to other facets of a party:
A. It is wise to have the guests wear nametags during the party.
B. Whether it is an adult, older child or teenager, there should always be another person to help at a party.

C. To preserve birthday presents, put them away in a safe place immediately after they are opened.

D. The present your child takes to a party should be one that he is proud to give.

BOOKS FOR CHAPTER ELEVEN

Here are some books that will give you some more ideas for special parties. The books listed at the end of Chapter Seven are also good books for you to refer to when planning a party.

Betty Crocker's Parties for Children, Lois M. Freeman. New York: Golden Press, 1974.

Creative Recreation Programming Handbook: Ideas and Year-Round Activities for Children and Youth, Dr. Adah Parker Strobell. Arlington, Va.: National Recreation and Park Association, 1971.

Five Hundred Games, Peter L. Cave. New York: Grosset & Dunlap, 1973.

Hallowe'en Cookbook, Susan Purdy. New York: Franklin Watts, 1977.

How to Give a Party, Jean and Paul Frame. New York: Franklin Watts, 1972.

Let's Celebrate: Holiday Decorations You Can Make, Peggy Parish. New York: William Morrow & Co., 1976.

New Year's to Christmas: Hooray Days, Things to Make and Do, Judith Ghinger. New York: Golden Press, 1977.

Popular Party Games, Alison M. Abel, editor. New York: Grosset & Dunlap, 1973.

A Pumpkin in a Pear Tree: Creative Ideas for Twelve Months of Holiday Fun, Ann Cole, Carolyn Haas, Elizabeth Heller, and Betty Weinberger. Boston: Little, Brown & Co., 1976.

Seasonal and Holiday Happenings, Joy Wilt and Terre Watson. Waco, Tex.: Educational Products Division, Word, Inc., 1978.

Star-Spangled Birthdays, Pasadena Symphony Juniors. Los Angeles: Read & Co., 1971.

12. "How Much Longer Till We Get There?"

"Get your things and hop in the car. We're going on a family outing!"

"Yay!" the children shout as they hustle out the door.

Once on the road, all goes well until the first child pipes up, "How much longer till we get there?"

From that point on, everything is uphill! The car suddenly gets crowded, the kids start to fight, and someone inevitably gets carsick.

"Is it worth it?" parents end up asking themselves.

I think I can answer this question. Family vacations and outings are worth it only if parents are fully equipped to combat what I call "CC" (car claustrophobia). Boredom is the major cause of CC, and its symptoms are whining, bickering, and fighting. Car claustrophobia is the number-one killer of family vacations and outings.

Preparing for Travel

It didn't take Bruce and me long to discover that by treating

163

the cause of CC we could usually get out of its symptoms. At first we tried the usual traveling games and activities. These things entertained the kids, but they exhausted us, so other remedies had to be found.

The two things we came up with were a smashing success. The first was the "car suitcase." For our family, the car suitcase is a small wooden suitcase that Bruce built. Its top side serves as a working surface. Both children have their own suitcase containing a variety of books, games, toys, etc. I go through each one approximately every four months to replace broken things and the things that the children have outgrown or gotten tired of. (Birthday gifts, Christmas stocking stuffers and Easter basket goodies are usually purchased with this suitcase in mind.)

The children know that their suitcases are never to leave the car. (The cases are stored in the trunk.) This is so the books, games, and toys will not get overused.

Through the years I've found that some items are better for car suitcases than others. The things I recommend are (listed in alphabetical order):

> Cardboard items to punch out and assemble
> Coloring books
> Colored pencils
> Construction toys with interlocking pieces
> Crossword puzzles
> Dot-to-dot books
> Fisher-Price movie viewer and reels
> Game and activity books
> Gummed paper shapes and stickers
> Magic slate
> Magnets and magnetic boards
> Miscellaneous puzzles and brain-teasers
> Paper dolls
> Pencils
> Picture books
> Playing cards
> Pocket dolls (with clothes or other equipment)

Rubber stamps with an ink pad
Rub-on transfers
Small chalk board and chalk
Small games
Small transportation toys (cars, trucks, trains, etc.)
Stencils and templates
Sticker books
Tablets of paper
View-Master and reels
Watercolor pens (crayons may melt if stored in the car
    trunk)
Wooden puzzles.

An old suitcase, a box, a large tote bag, or a drawstring bag can be used in place of a wooden suitcase. If you use one of these things, you may need to provide your child with a surface to work on. In this case, get a piece of Masonite from a lumber or hardware store. Masonite is lightweight, makes a great lap board, and can be stored with the car suitcase in the trunk of a car.

Another successful CC remedy has been our "tape set." One Christmas, Santa gave our family an inexpensive cassette tape recorder. We put it in a box along with Christopher's and Lisa's cassette tapes (the ones that come with story books). These tapes can be purchased at most toy, record, and department stores, and children of all ages like them. When Chris and Lisa aren't playing with the things in their suitcase, they are listening to their tapes. It really works out well!

Incidentally, we learned the hard way to keep an extra set of batteries for the tape recorder in the tape set. You may want to do the same.

The car suitcase and tape set are so successful we seldom have to resort to other things to keep our kids occupied. However, once in a while, for variety's sake, we do one of the following:

Encourage the children to observe certain objects en
    route.
Sing together.

Play games (many books about travel games can be purchased at toy, stationery, book and department
stores).

Conduct a family meeting.

Fantasize together (i.e., "If I had a million dollars, I
would—," "If I could be an animal, I would be—").

Take turns telling riddles and jokes.

Read to each other.

Take turns telling stories.

Do Mad Libs (Mad Lib books can be purchased at toy,
stationery, book and department stores).

And if all else fails, we encourage our children to *sleep!*
Car blankets are also kept in the trunk of the car along with
the suitcases and tape set. Bruce and I feel that all of these
things are as important as a spare tire.

Speaking of spare tires—one Christmas Eve at 11:00 P.M.,
Bruce and I were going "over the meadow and through the
woods to Grandmama's house" (well, in reality, we weren't
going over a meadow; we were driving on an isolated road-
way, and instead of snow, it was rain). The children were already there since they had spent the previous week with their
grandparents. Anyway, our "sleigh" had a flat tire, and we
didn't have a spare! Just as any other mature adult would do,
we panicked! Following the usual "It's all your fault" and "I
told you so!" arguments, we pulled ourselves together and
took some immediate steps to solve the problem. We got out
of the car and walked several miles in the rain until we came
to a truck stop. To make a long story short, we eventually
made it to Grandma's house, but it was not until 5:00 P.M. the
next day. Did our little episode teach Bruce and me a lesson?
It sure did! With every muddy step we took, we vowed never
to leave home again without the "basic necessities."

In addition to spare tires, there are other things that need
to be taken along on family vacations and outings. Something
to eat and drink are high on the "necessity list" if you won't
have access to stores or restaurants. Snacks that do not require

refrigeration are best. If the snack you choose will soil your child's hands and face, you may want to bring along a dozen or more damp paper towels (stored in a plastic bag so they won't dry out). These can be thrown away after your child has used them to clean his face and hands.

In regard to beverages: Small cans of fruit juice or punch can be frozen the night before a trip and thawed en route. In approximately two hours, you'll have an icy-cold drink without having the bother of an ice chest. Of course water is the best thing to quench a person's thirst. If you do not have a Thermos or simply don't want to hassle with one, try filling a disposable plastic milk bottle with crushed ice, then adding water. Again, you'll have an ice cold drink just about the time someone says, "I'm thirsty!" The good thing about using cans of juice and plastic containers is that these things can easily be disposed of.

Besides food and drink, you'll need some first-aid supplies. These can be kept in a medical supplies kit in the trunk of your car. If you put your own kit together, you may want to include some or all of these items (listed alphabetically):

Antibiotic salve
Antiseptic
Aspirin, Tylenol, or similar product
Bandaids
Basic splinting supplies
Disposable ammonia inhalants
Medication for motion sickness
Pepto Bismol (or something comparable)
Scissors
Snake-bite kit
Spoon
Sterile dressings and bandages
Sunburn lotion
Thermometer
Tourniquet
Triangular bandage

Traveling in Cars

Some time ago I supervised a Children and Travel Survey in which 104 children were asked questions about traveling, vacations and outings. Of these, 89 indicated that they "hated to ride in cars for a long time." When asked why, they gave answers like:

"My bottom gets tired."

"It gets boring."

"My parents get grumpy."

"Cars go too slow. They don't get you there fast enough."

"I hate sitting all the time."

"There's nothing to do."

These responses made sense. Children hate being confined to small areas. In addition, their short attention span makes it extremely difficult for them to sit for long periods of time. No wonder they balk at going on long trips in cars.

"But what if a car is the only way to get to Grandma's house? What then?" the interviewer asked. Most of the children answered, "I'd ask Grandma to come to my house!"

If only life was that simple! But it isn't, and sometimes it becomes necessary for everyone to "bite the bullet." When this happens and long trips in the car are absolutely essential, parents can make traveling easier for children (and themselves) by doing the following:

1. Make sure there are plenty of rest stops along the way. During each stop, encourage your child to get out of the car and move around. Also make sure that he visits the rest room.

2. When traveling cross-country, try to stop driving by 4:00 P.M. so that your child will have some time to play and unwind before he has to go to bed.

3. If you are traveling during the summer, make sure that your car is air-conditioned.

4. If you are traveling during the winter, make sure that your car has a heater.

Traveling in Planes, Trains, and Buses

In addition to the information about cars, the Children and Travel Survey revealed that most of the children preferred to take an airplane when traveling cross-country. Why? "Because it's exciting and it's fast!" they told us. Trains were their second choice, mostly because "the passengers are able to get up and move around." As for buses, children who rode one to school every day tended to put buses at the bottom of the list. Others reasoned that they didn't like buses for the same reasons they didn't like cars.

But whether your child takes an airplane, train, or bus to get where he's going, there will be a short period of time when he will need to be entertained. The car suitcase, the tape set, and the traveling games and activities can be adapted to these situations.

Motion Sickness

Remember hearing this verse when you were a kid?

Hasten, Jason!
Bring the basin!
Ooops, stop—
Bring the mop!

Well, it's still around! I heard it recently from one of the children in Lisa's class. I was asked to drive for a field trip and on the way to where we were going, one of the kids threw up in the car. It was terrible!

When a child gets carsick, everyone suffers. Parents would be well advised to do whatever they can to prevent carsickness. If you have a child who tends to get sick when he travels, see your doctor and get a medication for him. Chances are your child will outgrow his tendency toward motion sickness, but until then, as the old saying goes, "it's better to be safe than sorry!"

Child-Centered Vacations and Outings

During the Children and Travel Survey, we asked the participants to make two lists—one of "fun places to go" and the other of "not-so-fun places to go."

Almost every child included at least one of the following on his "fun places to go" list (in alphabetical order):

Amusement parks
Beach
Bike trails
Bowling alleys
The circus
The desert
Farms
Forests
Horseback riding
Lakes
Miniature golf courses
Mountains
Parks
Rivers
Skating rinks
Swimming pools
Theaters
The zoo

When asked, "What makes a place fun?" some of the children answered:

"It's made for kids."
"You get to do something, not just look at things."
"It's not boring."
"You can move around. You can run and play."
"You can get dirty and no one cares."
"People talk to you. You feel like you're a part of things."
"No one yells at you not to do something."
"It's not scary. It's safe."

These are only a few of the answers we received, but they are typical. Most of the responses to the question, "What makes a place fun?" reflected a need for:

1. Child-centeredness—places and activities that are geared toward children.
2. Involvement—activities that children can become involved in physically, mentally, or emotionally.
3. Variety—places that offer changing environments or a variety of activities.
4. Space—places where there is enough space for children to explore and move around in.
5. Social interaction—places where the children are a part of positive social interaction.
6. Safety—places where children can feel safe.

It would be wise for parents to take these things into consideration when planning a family vacation or outing. If vacations and outings would fulfill these basic needs, chances are their child will respond very favorably and the vacation or outing would be a smashing success.

In addition to choosing the right places, parents should avoid taking their children to the wrong places.

Adult-Centered Vacations and Outings

When making a list of the "not-so-fun places to go," the children we interviewed came up with:

Banks
Homes where there aren't any other children to play with
Offices
Places where you "just look at things" (museums and typical sightseeing spots)
Restaurants
Stores
Waiting rooms

My first recommendation in regard to these "not-so-fun places" is that you avoid taking your children to them. These places are for adults, and children are like "fish out of water" in them.

Eating out, shopping, sightseeing, visiting with other adults, etc., are adult pastimes. Children can tolerate these things in small doses only.

Parents who plan to pursue these activities are better off getting babysitters for their children. They will be able to function more efficiently and effectively, and their children will not have to suffer through boring experiences.

Whenever it is absolutely necessary to "drag the kids along," parents need to remember that boredom can lead to misbehavior. Again, the car suitcase and the tape set can help out in these situations. But whatever a parent does, he should avoid forcing a child to sit quietly for more than fifteen minutes with nothing to do. As one third-grade boy put it, "I only get in trouble when there's nothing else to do!"

Souvenirs

"Why does my child always want to buy something every time we go on a vacation or outing?" parents ask. The answer is simple. Children, like adults, want to make a good thing last as long as they can. Souvenirs help make this possible. For example, Lisa played with the baton she got at the circus long after the event was over. The baton served a valuable purpose as an extension of her experience at the circus.

Souvenirs help ease the pain of saying goodbye to a special place. They also ease the pain of experiencing the end of something exciting. I feel that souvenirs are *not* an "optional part of the program," and that parents need to include the cost of souvenirs in their budget when planning family vacations and outings.

This is not to say that children should be allowed to buy anything they want, any time they want! The following guidelines can make the whole souvenir experience a positive one.

1. Allot enough money for your child to buy a substantial souvenir. Flimsy things that do not work or break easily are a waste of money!
2. Before you arrive at your destination, tell your child

exactly how much you will be giving him to spend on a souvenir. (Remind him that he can add his own money to the sum if he wants to buy something that is more expensive.)

3. Encourage your child to wait until it's almost time to go home to buy his souvenir. This is so the souvenir will not get lost or broken during the outing. In addition, the child will have been exposed to all of his choices before he buys.

If your child is unsure that he will be getting a souvenir, he will beg and plead for it all during the outing. On the other hand, if he feels confident that he will eventually get a souvenir, everyone can relax and enjoy the total experience.

Memories or Nightmares

As with everything else in life, family vacations and outings can either create good memories or produce nightmares. It's up to the people who plan and conduct them! So, if you want your child's reflections to be positive ones, think before you travel.

By carefully planning your family's vacations and outings, you'll be able to look forward to the time when you and your child will reminisce together. "Remember the time we—."

SUMMARY

A. Family vacations and outings can be positive experiences if parents overcome the boredom that causes children to whine, bicker and fight.

B. To overcome boredom, parents can provide their children with:
   1. A car suitcase (a suitcase containing books, games, toys, etc.).
   2. A tape set (a set containing an inexpensive cassette

tape recorder, cassette story tapes and batteries for the
tape recorder).

3. A variety of games and activities.

C. Other things to take along on a trip include:

1. Car blankets.

2. Refreshments that do not require refrigeration.

3. Water and beverages in disposable containers.

4. A medical supplies kit.

D. Children do not like to ride in cars for a long period of
time.

1. They do not like being confined to small areas.

2. Their short attention span makes it difficult for them to
sit for long periods of time.

E. Traveling by car can be "less painful" for children if
parents make sure that:

1. There are plenty of rest stops.

2. They stop driving by 4:00 P.M.

3. The car is air-conditioned for summer travel.

4. The car is heated for winter travel.

F. Generally speaking, children prefer airplanes for cross-
country traveling. Trains are their second choice and cars
and buses are their last choice.

G. Parents of a child who tends to get car-sick may want to
obtain a medication (approved by a doctor) for the child.

H. A place is considered by children to be "fun" if it:

1. Is child-centered.

2. Involves the child.

3. Provides change and variety.

4. Provides enough space.

5. Is safe.

6. Provides positive social interaction.

I. A place is considered by children to be "not-so-fun" if it
involves adult pastimes like:

1. Eating out.

2. Shopping.

3. Sightseeing.

4. Visiting other adults.
J. Parents who want to engage themselves in adult pastimes are better leaving their children at home so that they can function more efficiently and effectively and their children will not have to suffer through boring experiences.

BOOKS FOR CHAPTER TWELVE

If you're interested in games for traveling, try this book: *Games for Children While Traveling* by Sid Hedges (New York: Grosset & Dunlap, 1973).

13. The "Susie, Eat Your Peas!" Syndrome

Don't ask me how or why it happened because I'm not sure that I could give you an answer; all I know is that one day I woke up to the stark realization that I was fifty pounds overweight. The "slap in the face" that woke me up and made me face my fat was an eight-year-old boy who was a part of a self-actualization class that I was teaching. Immediately following a class session that specifically dealt with human potential, this boy approached me and kindly said, "You know, Joy, you have the potential to be pretty, but you're too fat." If it weren't for the fact that I knew the boy extremely well (I knew that he loved me and wasn't out to get me), I would have been angry and very defensive, but under the circumstances (we had been together for two years and liked each other very much) I was crushed. Oh! how true it is! Sometimes the truth hurts.

For some time after this incident I tried rationalizing my fat away by reassuring myself that "beauty is only skin deep" and I had more to offer the world than beauty! But no matter how hard I tried I couldn't forget the words of my eight-year-old friend.

How could I inspire children and parents to utilize their potential to the fullest when I wasn't utilizing mine?

To make a long story short—

I got to the place where I couldn't cover up my fifty pounds of fat with clothes (the fashions that year were "fitted" instead of "blousy"). I couldn't stand myself any longer. So I began the long, arduous process of losing weight. After eight months of sheer agony, I finally shed the fifty pounds of "ugly fat." So what does all of this have to do with children and food? Plenty!

During the eight months I dieted I studied food and I learned a lot. The most valuable thing that I learned was the fact that *food needs to be understood and respected because of its tremendous potential to either help or hurt the human body.*

I had not understood or respected food and as a result I had used it to harm my body instead of help it.

From the very beginning children need to understand and respect food so that they can use it to help their bodies instead of hurt them.

Knowing how the various foods affect the body is important if a child is to utilize food properly. Thus children should be exposed to nutritional facts and concepts as early as possible.

Nutrition

When teaching nutrition to children I try to make the basic facts as simple as possible. This is what I tell children about nutrition:

"A human being needs good food.

"Too much of some foods hurts human beings rather than helps them.

"Good food makes it possible for human beings to stay alive and grow.

"Every human being needs protein. Protein helps the body grow, become strong, and stay well. Some foods that give us protein are milk, cheese, eggs, beef, veal, pork, lamb, fish, poultry, dried peas, dried beans, lentils and nuts.

"Every human being needs carbohydrates. Carbohydrates give the body energy (the strength or eagerness to work and do things). Some foods that give us carbohydrates are fruits, sugar, corn, rice, potatoes, bread, cereal and noodles.

"Every human being needs fats. Fats give the body energy and certain vitamins. Fats also keep the skin smooth and healthy. Some foods that give us fats are vegetable oils, cream, butter, margarine, mayonnaise and bacon.

"Every human being needs fiber. Fiber helps the body digest its food. It also contributes to healthy gums and clean teeth. Some foods that give us fiber are raw fruits, vegetables and whole-grain cereals.

"Every human body needs vitamins. Vitamins help the body grow. They also regulate the things that the body does and they help prevent certain sicknesses and diseases. Some foods that give us vitamins are milk, eggs, wheat-germ oil, yeast, fruits, vegetables, cereal, meat, fish, liver and nuts.

"Every human body needs minerals. Minerals help the body form teeth and bones. They also regulate the heart's action and help the blood form clots whenever a person is cut. Some foods that give us minerals are milk, cheese, eggs, meat, liver, dried fruit, seafood, vegetables (especially the green leafy ones) and salt.

"In order to stay alive and grow, you need to eat food that will give your body:

    Protein
    Carbohydrates
    Fats
    Fiber
    Vitamins
    Minerals.

"To make sure that your body is getting enough of the right

foods, you need to eat the following things every day:

   2 fruits (one should be a citrus fruit)
   2 vegetables (one should be a dark green or deep yellow)
   3 or more cups of milk
   2 or more servings of either cheese, eggs, beef, veal, pork,
      lamb, fish, poultry, dried beans, dried peas, lentils or
      nuts
   4 or more servings of whole grain, enriched or restored
      bread or cereal."

Although teaching children nutritional facts and concepts is important, it is just the beginning to good nutrition.

Shopping for Food

It is not enough for children to know about the kinds and quantities of food they should be eating. They need to have these foods available to them. This is where parents really come into the picture.

One thing I heard constantly while I was dieting was, "Dieting begins at the market." This is true! A parent can effectively control much of what a child eats by what he buys at the store. Children tend to eat the foods they have access to. If they have access to good food they will eat good food. If they have access to junk food they will eat junk food. Thus, parents should buy only those foods they want their children to eat. To make sure this happens, I recommend that parents:

1. Make their shopping list (based on sound nutritional principles) before they go to the market and avoid buying things that are not on the list.

2. Avoid taking their children with them to the market because children, who are vulnerable to advertisements and marketing strategies, will often persuade their parents to buy the wrong kinds of foods. Also, it is extremely frustrating for children to be surrounded by tantalizing snacks and foods that they cannot have.

Snacks

Once the food is home, then what? Is it "every man for himself—first come, first served"? I hope not. Improper snacking is one of the biggest reasons for children not eating the food that is placed before them at meal time.

I got my first clue that something was wrong when, two days after I had bought enough snacks to last our family of four for one week, the snacks were completely gone. Without realizing what was happening, I found myself going to the market at least three or four times a week. I excused the pattern that was developing by telling myself that my family was growing and naturally required more food. But when I stopped long enough to think about what was happening, I discovered how out of control our food situation had gotten.

No wonder my kids were turning their noses up at the meals that I was preparing for them. By the time they got to the dinner table they were stuffed. My children were literally snacking themselves into poor health and I was not only standing by and letting it happen—I was supplying the food! One thing that had helped perpetuate my actions was the sick affirmation I received from my children and their friends when they told me that I was a "neat mother because I let my kids eat anything they wanted, any time they wanted."

I finally came to my senses and decided to do something to correct the situation. My first step was to have Bruce put a lock on the cupboard that contained all of the snacks.

You can imagine how this went over with Chris and Lisa! The day the lock was installed they came home from school and, consistent with their daily pattern, headed immediately for the snack cupboard. Judging by the sounds that emanated from the kitchen, you would have thought that I had killed their best friend! If I had it to do over again, I think that I would have done things differently. I probably should have talked to them about the lock before it was installed, but I didn't, and there we were. Needless to say, a long heart-to-heart talk was in order.

That night during our family meeting, we talked about nothing else but food.

Chris and Lisa both reacted violently to the thought of having their snacking restricted. This had been anticipated, but it was still tough. After several hours of negotiation, we came up with the following rules.

1. No snacks will be permitted within two hours before meal times.
2. One snack will be permitted:

   mid-morning (between breakfast and lunch)

   mid-afternoon (between lunch and dinner)

   after dinner (if all the food served for dinner is tried and *if* a fair amount of food had been consumed at dinner, three small items (including a beverage) would be permitted)

Rule #1 was based on the belief that a snack eaten approximately two hours before mealtime will satisfy a child so that he can "make it" until mealtime but will not ruin his appetite for the meal. Rule #2 was based on the concept that children function better when they have five small meals a day. Their small stomachs cannot hold very much food at one time. Also, their high metabolic rate utilizes their food quickly.

These rules were written up and posted on the refrigerator door to serve as a reminder to everyone.

At first our snacking program was difficult for the whole family. Lisa and Chris went through a period of withdrawal, and it was hard for Bruce and me to stand by and watch (I felt like such a mean mother). But again, perseverance triumphed.

One thing that made the whole thing easier was that Bruce and I committed ourselves to providing snacks that would contribute to a total "balanced diet" for our children. Here is a list from our files of the snacks with which our family has experienced a great deal of success. It incorporates the results of my asking many children, "What is your favorite snack?" Of course, pies, pastries, cakes, cookies, pop, and candy were almost every child's first choice, but I think that there are some healthier alternatives, so I omitted the usual "junk foods" from this list.

Snacks (listed in alphabetical order):

Applesauce on graham crackers

Celery (stuffed with peanut butter or cheese spread)

Cereal and milk

Cheese

Cider, hot

Cottage cheese

Fruit, fresh, served plain or with cheese, yogurt, cottage cheese or cream (favorite fruits include apples, apricots, berries, cherries, grapes, melons, oranges, pears, pineapple, and plums)

Fresh fruit frappé

Fruit juice

Fruit juice, frozen in bars

Fruit leather

Graham crackers and honey butter or peanut butter

Granola

Ice cream

Kefir

Luncheon meats (served plain)

Milk, flavored

Milkshakes

Nuts

Peanut-butter balls rolled in peanuts or other nuts

Popcorn

Pretzels

Olives

Vegetables, raw, served plain or with dip or yogurt (favorite raw vegetables include broccoli buds, carrot sticks or curls, cauliflower flowers, celery sticks or curls, cherry tomatoes, cucumber sticks or slices, potato slices, radishes, zucchini sticks)

Vegetable juice

Yogurt, frozen or unfrozen

Please do not interpret my deleting the junk foods from this list as a statement against children partaking in junk foods. I believe it is a mistake to say that a child can *never* have junk foods. Parents who do this usually end up with children who develop a fixation on junk foods. These children, when they get away from their parents, can never seem to get enough sweets and goodies. On the other hand, children who are allowed to indulge occasionally usually take it in stride. If you are providing creative alternatives to junk food most of the time and allowing your child to eat candy canes at Christmas, Easter eggs on Easter, and birthday cake at parties, chances are he'll not become a "junk-food-aholic." Moderation and self-control are the key here, not total abstinence.

Meals

Did our snacking program have an effect on our mealtime? It sure did. In some ways there was less nagging because the kids were hungrier at meal time and consequently ate better. But getting the snacks organized did not stop the kids from spilling their milk or sneaking food to the dog under the table. Thus the list on the refrigerator was expanded to include the following mealtime rules:

1. Everyone will eat dinner together.
2. No one will leave the table before he has finished eating his meal.
3. Whenever a person has finished his meal he can leave the table even if everyone else is not finished eating.
4. Everyone will be served a portion of every food that is prepared for the meal (even if it is only one bite)
    —Each person can decide how big his portions will be.
    —No one should request more food than he will eat.
    —Additional helpings are permitted as long as the food holds out.
5. There will be no arguing or fighting at the dinner table.

People who break this rule will be asked to leave the table.

6. There will be no nagging at the dinner table; no saying "eat your food" or "clean up your plate."
7. Everyone must take his vitamin pill at the dinner table.
8. Mom will prepare food from a list agreed upon by the family.

Some of these rules may sound crazy, so please allow me to explain.

Rule #1: Everyone will eat dinner together. We formulated this rule because we realized that the dinner hour was the only time in the day when our family was all together.

Rule #2: No one will leave the table before he has finished eating his meal. The rule was decided upon because of all the interruptions that would happen just about the time we sat down for dinner. The phone would ring, a friend would knock at the door, one of the children had to go to the bathroom. Someone would remember that he left the water running in the bathroom, etc., etc., etc. Dinnertime was like a three-ring circus.

The only way to remedy the situation was to take the phone off the hook, refuse to answer the door (after explaining to the kids in the neighborhood that Chris and Lisa could not play during the dinner hour), and then ask, before everyone sat down, "Is everyone ready to begin?" (This meant, have you gone to the bathroom; have you washed your hands; have you done everything that needs to be done?) It was amazing how this rule eliminated the confusion that was previously associated with the dinner hour.

Rule #3: Whenever a person has finished his meal, he can leave the table, even if everyone else is not finished eating.

It got to be ridiculous. Bruce and I were rushing through our meal just so that the whole family could reach the "finish line" at the same time. Bruce is a slow eater, Chris is a fast eater, and Lisa and I are somewhere in between. It was impossible to synchronize the time it took all of us to eat a meal.

Besides, Bruce and I enjoyed lingering at the dinner table and talking. To Chris and Lisa this was a bore. Allowing everyone to leave the table when he was finished eating freed each person to eat his food at a pace that was comfortable to him.

Incidentally, I have tried to slow down when it comes to eating, and I have encouraged both of my kids to do the same. Nutritionists point out, and we have found it true, that it takes less food to make a person "feel full" when the food is eaten slowly. People who "inhale" their food seldom experience the pleasure and satisfaction that comes from tasting the food and consequently seldom feel satisfied. This is why they continue to eat and eat and eat.

Rule #4: Everyone will be served a portion of every food that is prepared for the meal (even if it is only one bite). This rule was based on the old "try it, you'll like it" adage. It was hoped that by trying new things Chris and Lisa would expand their tastes to encompass a wide variety of foods. After all, anything gets old fast when it is served over and over again. If children are to remain interested in eating, they need to like, and be served, a variety of foods. Thus it behooves parents to encourage their children to explore new foods.

I hate leftovers and Bruce hates throwing food away. Consequently we found ourselves in a real bind. I was doling out huge servings of food to avoid having leftovers and Bruce was forcing the kids to "clean up their plates" to avoid throwing the food away. The kids were complaining because they felt they were being forced to eat too much, and they were right. To resolve our dilemma, Bruce and I agreed to let Chris and Lisa decide how much of each food they would be served.

We encourage them to avoid having "eyes bigger than their stomachs." We ask them to start with small portions and request more if they want it. This usually works pretty well.

Rule #5: There will be no arguing or fighting at the dinner table. People who break this rule will be asked to leave the table.

Bruce and I insisted on this rule—mainly to preserve our

sanity! Nothing gets to either one of us more than the bickering and fighting that takes place between Chris and Lisa.
Whenever their verbal warfare began at the dinner table,
Bruce and I would find ourselves wrapping food around the
knots in our stomachs instead of eating. Because of Rule #2,
we were unable to walk away from the turmoil (which is
ordinarily what we try to do) so we decided to squelch it—
at least until after dinner.

Chris and Lisa are not always pleased with this rule, but
they consented in order to get Rule #6 on the list.

Rule #6: There will be no nagging at the dinner table; no
demands to "eat your food" or "clean up your plate."

This was the rule both Chris and Lisa held out for. Our
nagging had really started to get to them.

The rules about snacking and eating meals were clear now,
and Chris and Lisa did not want (or need) to be continually
reminded of them. We agreed, and the nagging stopped.

Before I go on to the seventh rule, let me say that the
"clean up your plate" syndrome that our society forced its
children into is, according to many diet experts, one of the
primary causes of America's overweight problems. Adults
have gotten into the habit of cleaning up their plates and will
eat everything in sight—even if they don't want or need it!

Another reason for overweight people in America is the
"don't waste your food" syndrome. People become human
garbage cans in an effort to avoid wasting food. They will eat
anything and everything that's available just so they will not
have to throw it out.

I do not advocate that we waste food in order to stay slim.
But I do advocate serving smaller portions. I also advocate
encouraging children to eat only until they are full instead of
making them eat until all of their food is gone.

Rule #7: Everyone must take his vitamin pill at the dinner
table. This rule was for Bruce's sake. He tends to be a
"nervous Nelly" when it comes to making sure that the kids
are getting all of their vitamins and minerals. A balanced

diet should be sufficient, but it's difficult making sure that everyone gets exactly the right combination of things. So just to be on the safe side, we invested in some good multiple vitamins. They're distributed at the dinner hour so that everyone is sure to get one. Bruce rests easier now and the children claim they feel better. Everyone seems to be pleased with this rule.

Rule #8: Mom will prepare food from a list agreed upon by the family.

"We don't eat the food you fix because we don't like it!" Chris announced at a family meeting. Lisa agreed, and I was crushed. Based on their daily responses at the dinner table, I half expected a negative response to my question, "Why don't you eat the food I fix for you?" I never served a meal without having at least one of them say, "Not this again!" or "Why don't you ever fix something that's good?"

In all fairness, I had to admit that I had not been very concerned about preparing meals that appealed to my children. Rather, they were designed to please Bruce and me, and I hoped that the children would catch on. I rationalized my behavior by telling myself that the food I was preparing was nutritious and that Chris and Lisa should be eating it.

Well, it just didn't work out that way. It was true that Bruce and I loved my meals. (And we didn't mind cleaning up the food that Chris and Lisa left behind.) But the children weren't eating, and Bruce and I were fast becoming baby blimps.

What should we do?

Chris came up with a suggestion: "Why don't you fix food we like?" His suggestion sounded reasonable. So we sat down and made a list of Chris and Lisa's favorite foods. I promised to prepare meals that consisted of some, if not all, foods from the list. Of course, Bruce and I had to put our foot down on things like root beer, candy bars, popsicles, and the like. So the list we use does not include *everything* the kids would choose if they had free rein.

I've combined Chris and Lisa's list with one that was prepared by the same group of children who came up with the snack list. I'm including it in this book in the hope that you may use it as a starting point to formulate a similar list for your own family.

Please note: I have not included recipes here because some parents prefer to use health foods while others do not. Either way, all of the things on this list can be prepared with or without the use of natural foods.

Breakfast Foods (listed in alphabetical order):

Bacon

Bagels

Biscuits

Breads (banana, carrot, pineapple bread, etc.)

Cereal, cold with milk

Cereal, hot

Cheese blintzes

Cinnamon toast

Cocoa, hot

Corn fritters

Cornbread and honey

Eggs, hard-boiled, scrambled, poached, fried, or baked

Eggs in the hole (egg fried in the center of a slice of bread from which a circle has been removed)

Eggnog

French toast

Fruit, fresh

Grapefruit and honey

Grits

Ham

Hamburger patty

Luncheon meats, fried

Muffins

Pancakes

Potato pancakes

Sausage

Waffles

Main Dishes (listed in alphabetical order):

Baked beans

Barbecued pork or beef ribs

Cheeseburgers

Chicken, fried, broiled, barbecued, or baked (children usually prefer the drumsticks, thighs, and breasts)

Chicken salad

Chili

Chili dogs (hot dogs on a bun with chili poured over the top)

Creamed chipped beef over toast

Deviled eggs

Eggs, hard-boiled, scrambled, poached, fried or baked

Egg sandwich

Enchiladas

Fish sticks

Grilled cheese sandwich

Ham

Ham loaf

Ham salad

Hamburgers

Hot dogs (plain or in a bun)

Lasagna

Luncheon meat or plain meat sandwich

Macaroni and cheese

Meat balls

Meat loaf

Peanut butter sandwiches (add honey, raisins, bananas, nuts, apples or prunes)

Pigs in a blanket (hot dogs, heated, wrapped in biscuit dough, and then baked for 15 minutes at 450°)

Pizza

Pork chops, fried, broiled, barbecued, or baked

Ravioli

Salisbury steaks

Sloppy joes (browned ground meat, seasoned with tomato sauce and spices, served on a hamburger bun; beans may be added)

Soup

Spaghetti

Stew

Tacos

Tortilla dogs (hot dogs, heated, wrapped in a flour tortilla with cheese and then baked for 15 minutes at 450°)

Tuna casserole

Tuna salad

Tuna sandwiches

Turkey

Favorite Vegetables (listed in alphabetical order):

Baked beans

Carrots (preferred glazed with butter and brown sugar)

Corn on the cob

Green beans

Pork and beans

Potatoes, steamed, mashed, baked, or fried

Refried beans

Rice

Yams (preferred with butter, brown sugar and pineapple)

Acceptable Vegetables (listed in alphabetical order)

Artichokes

Asparagus

Broccoli

Cabbage

Cauliflower

Peas

Squash

Fruits and Salads (listed in alphabetical order):

Applesauce

Baked apple

Carrot salad (especially good with pineapple, raisins or
   nuts added)

Fresh fruit and cottage cheese (fruits that go especially
   well with cottage cheese are melons, pineapple, and
   bananas)

Fresh spinach salad (a good way to get children to eat
   spinach)

Fruit salad (any combination of fresh or canned fruit
   will do)

Jello salad (to make it more nutritious, add yogurt or
   cottage cheese and fruit or vegetables before it is set)

Macaroni salad

Potato salad

Sliced tomatoes

Three-bean salad

Tossed green salad (especially good when garnished with
   grated cheese, small pieces of meat, nuts, fresh fruits
   and/or raw vegetables)

Waldorf salad (apples, celery, raisins, nuts and mayonnaise)

Serving foods your children like will make things a whole
lot easier on you—and your ego. It's affirming to the cook
when everyone enthusiastically dives into the food set before
them. It's also a great feeling when everyone leaves the table
exclaiming, "That sure was good!"

But what if the members in your family can't agree on what
they like or want for dinner? Then have everyone take turns
planning the meals. This can be done on either a daily or a
weekly basis. If everyone has an equal opportunity to plan a
meal, everyone will get exactly what they want part of the time.
This is about as fair as you'll ever be able to get.

And while you're letting your family help you plan the
meal, how about letting them help you prepare it? It's a proven
fact that children are more likely to eat food when they have
had a hand in preparing it. Some educators believe this hap-

pens because children want their endeavors to be successful and that refusing to eat their own cooking is admitting failure. Other educators say that seeing what goes into a casserole or another food product removes the mystery that often inhibits children from eating it. I'll never forget observing a child watching some apples change into applesauce. "Ooh!" the child squealed with delight. "The apples are growing into applesauce!" This same child had refused to eat applesauce before the cooking experience because she was never quite sure what it was. After she had experienced the fact that applesauce was merely apples in another form, applesauce became one of her favorite foods.

Now, you may not experience the same amount of success with eggplant, but anything is worth a try!

We live in a society that is food-oriented:

When we are happy, we eat.

When we are depressed, we eat.

When we are anxious, we eat.

When we are bored, we eat.

We eat when we are alone.

We eat when we are with people.

American people eat constantly, and their problems with overweight show it.

"Eat it today, wear it tomorrow," people joke. But in reality, it's not very funny.

So what do we do? Give up eating? Of course not.

We need to understand and respect food if we are going to use it to help us instead of hurt us. For some of us, this process did not start soon enough, and it's almost too late. But this isn't true for our children. What they eat today is what their bodies will be tomorrow. It would be wise for all of us parents to begin taking this fact more seriously.

SUMMARY

A. Children and adults alike need to understand and respect food and nutrition because of food's tremendous potential to either help or hurt the human body.

B. A balanced diet includes adequate amounts of:
   1. Protein.
   2. Carbohydrates.
   3. Fats.
   4. Fiber.
   5. Vitamins.
   6. Minerals.

C. To make sure that a child is getting enough of the right foods, he needs to eat the following things every day:
   1. Two fruits (one should be a citrus fruit).
   2. Two vegetables (one should be dark green or deep yellow).
   3. Three or more cups of milk.
   4. Four or more servings of either cheese, eggs, beef, veal, pork, lamb, fish, poultry, dried beans, dried peas, lentils or nuts.
   5. Four or more servings of whole-grain, enriched or restored bread or cereal.

D. When shopping for food, it is wise for parents to:
   1. Make their shopping list (based on sound nutritional principles) before they go to the market, and avoid buying things that are not on the list.
   2. Avoid taking their children with them to the market, because children, who are vulnerable to advertisements and marketing strategies, will often persuade their parents to buy the wrong kinds of foods.

E. Two good rules for snacking are:
   1. No snacks will be permitted within two hours before meal times.
   2. One snack will be permitted:
      a. Mid-morning (between breakfast and lunch).

    b. Mid-afternoon (between lunch and dinner).

    c. After dinner (if all the food served for dinner is tried, and *if* a fair amount of food has been consumed at dinner, three small items will be permitted).

F. Children should not be totally restricted from eating junk foods, as this may cause them to develop a fixation on junk foods.

G. Eight good rules for meal time are:

    1. Everyone will eat dinner together.

    2. No one will leave the table before he has finished eating his meal.

    3. Whenever a person has finished his meal, he can leave the table, even if everyone else is not finished eating.

    4. Everyone will be served a portion of every food that is prepared for the meal (even if it is only one bite).

    5. There will be no arguing or fighting at the dinner table. Anyone breaking this rule will be asked to leave the table.

    6. There will be no nagging at the dinner table; no saying "eat your food" or "clean up your plate."

    7. Everyone must take his vitamin pill at the dinner table.

    8. Mom will prepare food from a list agreed upon by the family.

H. Children should be encouraged to try new foods so that they will expand their taste to encompass a wider variety of food.

I. Children will respond better at mealtime if they are served food that they like. Thus it is strategic to bring children in on the meal planning.

J. Children are more likely to eat food that they have had a hand in preparing. Thus it is wise to involve children in the preparation of a meal.

BOOKS FOR CHAPTER THIRTEEN

As I mentioned earlier in the chapter, there are hundreds of good cookbooks out on the market for children. These are just a few of my favorites.

Betty Crocker's Cookbook for Boys and Girls. New York: Golden Press, 1977.

Cool Cooking, Esther Hautzig. New York: Lothrop, Lee & Shepard, 1973.

Creative Food Experiences for Children, Mary T. Goodwin and Gerry Pollen. Washington, D.C.: Center for Science in the Public Interest, 1974.

Crunchy Bananas, Barbara Wilms. Santa Barbara, Calif.: Sagamore Books, 1975.

Feed Me I'm Yours, Vicki Lansky. Wayzata, Minn.: Meadowbrook Press, 1975.

The Good For Me Cookbook, Karen B. Croft. San Francisco: R & E Research Associations, 1971.

Growing Food Growing Up, A Child's Natural Food Book, Esther Lewin and Birdina Lewin. Los Angeles: Ward Ritchie Press, 1973.

The Happy Pixies' Cookbook: Kitchen Fun for Little Cooks, Lon Amick. Kansas City, Mo.: Hallmark.

Help! My Child Won't Eat Right, A Guide to Better Nutrition, Antoinette Kuzmanich Hatfield and Peggy Smeeton Stanton. Washington, D.C.: Acropolis Books Ltd., 1974.

How to Make Elephant Bread, Kathy Mandry, Joe Toto. Pantheon Books, 1971.

Kids Are Natural Cooks, Roz Ault. Boston: Houghton-Mifflin, 1974.

The Kid's Cookbook, Yum! I Eat It, Patricia Petrich and Rosemary Dalton. Concord, Calif.: Nitty Gritty Productions, 1973.

Let's Give a Party, Susan Purdy. New York: Grosset & Dunlap, 1976.

The Mother Child Cook Book: An Introduction to Educational Cooking, Nancy J. Ferreira. Pacific Coast Publishers.

Natural Sweets and Treats, Ruth Laughlin. Santa Barbara, Calif.: Woodbridge Press Publishing Co., 1973.

The No-Cook Cookery Cookbook, Mary Jean Stangl. Self-published, 1976.

Peanuts and Popcorn, Julianne Lemon. Concord, Calif.: Nitty Gritty Productions, 1977.

Small World Cook and Color Book, Beverly Frazier. San Francisco: Troubador Press, 1971.

Taste and Smell! Joy Wilt and Terre Watson. Waco, Tex.: Educational Products Division, Word, Inc., 1978.

14. The Final Hour

Give yourself a gold star if you and your child have sur-
vived the day—but before you apply it to your achievement
list, there's one more "river to cross," one more "hurdle to
jump," one more "hoop to crawl through," and that's—bedtime. This is where most parents blow it.

You've rescued your child from the middle of the street,
you've refereed his fights, you've managed to ward off mal-
nutrition (for at least one more day), and you've helped your
child find his lost iguana. Already you have gone above and
beyond the call of duty. No wonder the urge to scream surges

197

through your body when your child calls out from his bed, "I need a drink of water."

Bedtime is rough on everyone. It's rough on the child, because, according to the children I've worked with:

1. A child doesn't like endings. He wishes that every good thing, especially daytime, could go on forever.
2. A child doesn't like good-byes. He doesn't like to say goodbye, even if it's only for a night.
3. A child doesn't like to be excluded. If he's in bed while someone else is up doing things, he feels left out.
4. A child doesn't want to miss anything. If the TV's still going and things are still happening, he fears he's going to miss out on something.

This is why children resist bedtime and this is what makes bedtime rough for parents. So what are we to do? We don't feel like putting a gold star on our achievement chart after a knock-down, drag-out fight with our child over bedtime.

I wish I could offer a few suggestions guaranteed to make a child beg to go to bed, but I can't. All I can do is tell you about some things that could possibly "ease the pain."

I'm going to present two different plans for handling bedtime. It's up to you to choose the one that will be best for your family.

There is a lot of debate over how to handle bedtime. Some people advocate that a child, like an adult, should be able to go to bed whenever he chooses. They feel that a child inwardly knows how much sleep he requires and will regulate his sleeping habits if he is left to do so.

For a short time Bruce and I tried this approach (Plan A) with Chris and Lisa and we experienced both good and bad things.

The goods things were:

There was no conflict between us and the children over bedtime.

The children assumed complete responsibility for getting

themselves to bed, so, in some ways, it was less hassle for Bruce and me.

The children loved it.

The bad things were:

It took a long time for the children to regulate themselves and while they were doing it they were cross and cranky. What they wanted to do (i.e., watch TV) usually won out over what was best for them (i.e., getting enough sleep).

Bruce and I did not have time to ourselves or with each other.

I'm sure that Plan A would produce a longer list of pros and cons if used over a long period of time. However, these are the ones we experienced.

Anyway, Plan A worked for our family, but not all that well, so we swung into Plan B. This approach, the more traditional of the two plans, is based on the concept that children need a regular bedtime and that parents need to help them establish and maintain it. Some people advocate that a child who is put to bed at the same time every night will get sleepy at the same time every night. Bruce and I have found this to be true with our children.

Here is how Plan B works:

Setting up the bedtime
1. Get together with your child and find out when he feels he should go to bed every night.
2. Negotiate with him until you arrive at a bedtime that will be acceptable to everyone (if the child cannot come to the point of using good judgment, parents may have to make the decision without his approval). The following chart may help you and your child establish an appropriate bedtime. (Please note: these figures are only approximate and should be adapted to every child and every situation.)

Child's age	Hours of sleep required in the morning	Hours of sleep required in the afternoon	Hours of sleep required at night	Suggested bedtime
Infant to 1 year	1–2 hours	1–2 hours	12 hours	7:00 or 8:00 P.M.
2–5 years	none	½–2 hours	12 hours	7:00 or 8:00 P.M.
6–9 years	none	none	10–11 hrs.	8:00 or 9:00 P.M.
10–12 years	none	none	8–9 hrs.	9:00 or 9:30 P.M.

3. Explain to your child that he will be going to bed every night at the same time (except on special occasions and possibly weekends; bedtime on these nights should be negotiated at least one day in advance).

Approaching bedtime
1. Approximately thirty minutes before bedtime, tell your child that he has ten minutes to finish doing whatever he is doing.
2. Approximately twenty minutes before bedtime, tell your child that it is time for him to get ready for bed.
3. Approximately five minutes before bedtime, make sure that your child is ready for bed and that
   a. He has gone to the bathroom.
   b. He has gotten a drink of water (if he wants one).
   c. He has gathered together everything he's going to take to bed with him (toys, books, Kleenex, security objects, etc.).
   d. He has kissed and said good night to whomever he wants to.

Of course, these time allotments will vary depending upon your child and upon what things he has to do to get ready for bed and how fast he can do them.

If your child is able to tell time, give him a watch or clock so that he can gauge his own time. Use a timer with a child who can't tell time.

Bedtime

1. Tell your child, "You have done and gotten everything that you need. Please do not get out of your bed and do not call for me because I will not come back into your room until you are asleep. I will check on you before I go to bed to make sure that you are all right." (This last sentence helps overcome his fear, "What if something happens to me while I'm lying here?")
2. Turn on the night light (if your child needs one).
3. Turn out the bedroom light.
4. Leave the room; then close the door (if this is acceptable to the child).
5. Don't come back, no matter how much he calls, screams, fusses or cries, until he has fallen asleep.

Some children find it difficult, if not impossible, to fall asleep the minute they get into bed. These children should be allowed to look at books or play quietly with toys in their bed until they drop off to sleep. Christopher often complains, "I'm not sleepy—I'll never be able to go to sleep!" "That's okay," we tell him, "you don't have to go to sleep. Just stay in bed and look at a book or play with one of your toys." It never fails; he's usually asleep in less than ten minutes. By telling him that he doesn't have to go to sleep, we remove the pressure and he can relax enough to fall asleep much more easily.

Bedtime Rituals

The procedure I have just described can become a very happy and satisfying bedtime ritual for your child. If this happens, you may find that he'll get extremely upset if you skip anything or change the order of events. It may seem complicated to get started, but bedtime rituals often pay off in the end. Everyone gets to the place where he knows exactly what to expect and he functions accordingly. However, beware! When you are in the process of establishing a bedtime ritual, make sure that you do not include things that you cannot consistently deliver. Things such as stories, games, or massages are nice, but only when they are done willingly on the part of the parent. It may not always be possible for you to tell your child a story or give him a massage before you put him to bed.

This is why I recommend that these activities take place some time in the evening *before* the bedtime ritual begins. When they are not considered to be part of the ritual, they will not be expected; instead, they will be appreciated if and whenever they happen.

Helpful Hints Regarding Bedtime

Over the years, I've gathered some helpful hints from fellow parents regarding bedtime. I've found them extremely accurate and helpful, so I'm going to share them with you at this time.

1. If your child takes a nap in the afternoon, make sure that he doesn't sleep too long if you want him to go to bed at his regular bedtime. If your child tends to be grumpy when he is awakened from a nap, wake him up indirectly by turning on a radio or TV, or by putting one of his favorite records on the record player.

2. Roughhousing is a stimulating activity and should be over long before the bedtime ritual begins. This is to give the child a chance to "unwind" before he has to go to bed.

3. Answer your child's question, "How come so-and-so gets to stay up longer than me?" by saying, "Every person is different and requires different things to keep his body alive

and well. You need more sleep than ———— and I love you
enough to make sure that you get it!"

4. If a child is tense and uptight, a warm bath or gentle
massage can help to calm him down.

5. Children should not be allowed to watch scary movies
or listen to ghost stories right before they go to bed, because
scary movies and ghost stories often cause nightmares.

6. If your child has gone to bed on time and has had a
good night's sleep, affirm him the next morning by saying
something like, "Today will probably be a good day for you
because you got plenty of sleep last night!"

Nightmares

As though getting your child to sleep isn't enough! Get
ready to chase ghosts out of closets and shoo snakes and alli-
gators out of the house, because if your child is normal, he'll
be calling on you to do it. What could possibly prompt him
to make such demands? His nightmares. They may sound silly
to you, but they're real to him and if anyone is going to get
any sleep, you're going to have to take them seriously.

What is the best way to handle nightmares? Try these suggestions taken from my book *Happily Ever After:*

Strive to
1. Be empathetic and understanding.
2. Find out what the nightmare is about so that you can
   "talk it through" with the child.
3. Return to the child's bedroom with him.
4. Take a tour of the bedroom (or the entire house, if
   necessary) with the child, showing him that all is safe.
5. Tuck the child back into bed.
6. Stay in the room with him until he is not afraid to stay
   alone or until he goes back to sleep.
7. Reassure him that you will be in your bedroom and that

he can call you or come and get you if he needs you again.

8. Sleep with the child or allow him to sleep with you *if* the nightmares persist on through the night.

Strive not to

1. Trivialize the nightmare by saying things like "That's silly! There are no snakes on the floor!" or "Don't be foolish! There are no such things as monsters!"
2. Send the child back to his room alone.
3. Leave the child before he feels good about your leaving.
4. Make the child stay in his room by himself if he is still frightened.
5. Take the child to bed with you immediately, before trying to resolve the nightmare for him. For everyone's sake, having the child come to bed with you should be the *last* resort.
6. Allow your child to watch movies or experience things that will cause him to have nightmares.

Sometimes your child may go through a stage where he is having nightmares every night. When this occurs, he may be frightened to go to bed. If his fear is genuine, try this routine:

First night. Sit on his bed until he falls asleep.

Second night. Stay in the room until he falls asleep. Sit somewhere further away from the bed.

Third night. Sit in the doorway where he can see you until he falls asleep.

Fourth night. Stay just outside his door (where he cannot see you) until he falls asleep.

Fifth night. Assure him that you will be in the house and that you can come to him if he should need you. Promise to check in on him before you go to bed.

Asleep at Last!

After your kids are sound asleep—do yourself a favor. Sit

down, prop up your feet and sip a hot cup of coffee or an ice-cold drink. You deserve it!

SUMMARY

A. A child does not like bedtime because he doesn't like:
   1. Endings.
   2. Goodbyes.
   3. Being excluded.
   4. Missing out on anything.
B. There are several ways to handle bedtime.
   1. *Plan A* allows a child, like an adult, to go to bed whenever he chooses. His body system inwardly knows how much sleep he requires and will regulate his sleeping habits if left to do so.
   2. *Plan B* is based on the concept that children need a regular bedtime and that parents need to help them establish and maintain it. This plan sets forth the idea that a child who is put to bed at the same time every night will get sleepy at the same time every night. Plan B offers guidelines for:
      a. Setting up the bedtime.
      b. Approaching bedtime.
      c. Bedtime.
C. Bedtime rituals become very important to children and they often become upset when parents try to skip anything or change the order of events.
D. Bedtime rituals can be a positive thing as everyone gets to the place where he knows exactly what to expect and functions accordingly.
E. When establishing a bedtime ritual, parents should only include those things they can consistently deliver.
F. Helpful hints regarding bedtime:
   1. Don't let your child nap too long during the day. Wake him up indirectly if necessary.

2. Avoid roughhousing with your child right before bedtime.
3. Tell your child: "Everyone is different and requires
   different amounts of sleep."
4. Do not allow your child to watch scary movies or listen
   to ghost stories right before bedtime.
5. Use a warm bath or gentle massage to calm down a
   child who is overly nervous or excited.
6. Affirm your child the next morning when he has gone
   to bed on time and gotten a good night's sleep.
G. Nightmares need to be taken seriously and dealt with.
   There are several things parents can do to help a child
   who has had a nightmare.
H. A child who has nightmares every night requires special
   attention.

Suggested Reading

When it comes to Big Bad Wolves, this book has dealt with some of the "Biggies," but it has not dealt with all of them.

If you are interested in helping your child cope with:

Self-concept
Basic needs
Problems and decisions
Emotions
Trauma
Sex education
Sex roles
Socialization

you may want to read my books *Happily Ever After* (Waco, Tex.: Word Books, 1977), *You're All Right, You're One of a Kind, Keeping Your Body Alive and Well, Mine and Yours, Handling Your Ups and Downs,* and *Saying What You Mean* (Waco, Tex.: Educational Products Division, Word, Inc., 1978).

If you are interested in helping your child cope with
 Rights
 Responsibilities
 Home
 Church
 School
 Friends
you may want to read my books *An Uncomplicated Guide to Becoming a Superparent* (Waco, Tex.: Word Books, 1977), *Making Up Your Own Mind,* and *A Kid's Guide to Making Friends* (Waco, Tex.: Educational Products Division, Word, Inc., 1979).

If you are interested in helping your child cope with
 Parents
 Siblings
 Grandparents
 Relatives
 Babysitters
 Family life
you may want to read my books *The Nitty-Gritty of Family Life, Needing Each Other,* and *Surviving Fights with Your Brothers and Sisters* (Waco, Tex.: Educational Products Division, Word, Inc., 1979).

In addition to the books I've written, I'd like to recommend the following:

Baby and Child Care, Dr. Benjamin Spock. New York: Pocket Books, 1968.

Between Parent and Child, Dr. Haim G. Ginott. New York: Avon Books, 1971.

Child Behavior from Birth to Ten, Frances L. Ilg, M.D., and Louise Bates Ames, Ph.D. New York: Harper and Row, 1955.

The Complete Question and Answer Book of Child Training, Esther Laden Cava, Ph.D. New York: Hawthorn Books, Inc., 1972.

How To Parent, Dr. Fitzhugh Dodson. New York: Signet, 1970.

The Mother's Almanac, Marguerite Kell and Elia Parsons. New York: Doubleday, 1975.

The Open Home: Early Learning Made Easy for Parents and Children. New York: St. Martin's Press, 1976.

I've heard that it's easier to kill a wild animal than it is to tame it. This is probably true. But what a waste to kill something that could possibly enhance and enrich your life!

No, don't try to kill the Big Bad Wolves. Instead, turn them into friends. When tame, they make faithful servants and marvelous companions.